Loss and Grief

Also available from M&K Publishing

All books can be ordered online at:
www.mkupdate.co.uk

Caring for Skills series

Interpersonal Skills
Bob Wright, SRN, RMN, MSc (Leeds)
ISBN: 978-1-905539-37-6
Published by M&K Update Ltd

Experienced professionals and novice care workers a like need to communicate meaningfully with their clients. To do so successfully you need to understand the skills required and how to practice them.

This workbook can be used as a stand-alone module or at your workplace as part of an assessment programme, or as part of a more formal training programme at a college or other institution. You can read it in parts, if this is more convenient for you, or you can interrupt your reading to do some of the exercises. There is space for you to keep notes. The workbook can be used in a very flexible way and covers a variety of skills required for effective communication.

Titles in print include:

Improving Patient Outcomes: a guide for ward managers
ISBN 978 -1-905539-06-1

Music Makes a Difference: A practical guide to developing music sessions with people with learning disabilities
ISBN 978 -1-905539-19-62

Forthcoming:

- COPD: diagnosis and management in hospital and the community
- Identification and treatment of alcohol dependency
- The Management of Pain in Older People Workbook
- Managing emotions in women's health
- Mood disorders in patients with COPD: detection and management
- Multi-disciplinary approach to young fathers
- Nutrition for children - A no nonsense guide for parents
- Pre-teen and teenage pregnancy: a 21st century reality

Loss and Grief

Bob Wright

SRN, RMN, Hon MSc (Leeds)

Loss and Grief
Bob Wright, SRN, RMN, MSc (Leeds)

ISBN: 978-1-905539-43-7

First published 1992
New updated edition 2007

British Library Catalogue in Publication Data
A catalogue record for this book is available from the British Library

Notice
Clinical practice and medical knowledge constantly evolve. Standard safety precautions must be followed, but, as knowledge is broadened by research, changes in practice, treatment and drug therapy may become necessary or appropriate. Readers must check the most current product information provided by the manufacturer of each drug to be administered and verify the dosages and correct administration, as well as contraindications. It is the responsibility of the practitioner, utilising the experience and knowledge of the patient, to determine dosages and the best treatment for each individual patient. Neither the publisher nor the authors assume any liability for any injury and/or damage to persons or property arising from this publication.

The Publisher
To contact M&K Publishing write to:
M&K Update Ltd · The Old Bakery · St. John's Street
Keswick · Cumbria CA12 5AS

Tel: 01768 773030 · Fax: 01768 781099
publishing@mkupdate.co.uk
www.mkupdate.co.uk

Designed & typeset in 11pt Usherwood Book by Mary Blood

Contents

ABOUT THE AUTHOR

Bob Wright SRN RMN HonMSc (Leeds)
Bob Wright was until recently a Clinical Nurse Specialist in crisis intervention in the Accident and Emergency Department at Leeds General Infirmary. He has developed his experience in counseling and as a workshop facilitator over a number of years, in this country as well as in Australia and the USA. He is the author of two other books Caring in Crisis and Sudden Death.

ACKNOWLEDGEMENTS

To the following who contributed and edited the original series:

OPEN LEARNING ADVISOR
Glennis Johnson BSc

EDITORS
Susan Bird BA (Nurs) RGN CCNS CertEd (FE) FRSH
David Rennie DYCS DSW CQSW

Introduction

The feelings and thoughts connected with loss, grief, dying and death have always concerned people. The questions raised by life and death, and attachments and loss, have resulted in countless books, poems and songs. The expression of grief is a universal response by which people adapt to a significant loss; the loss of something, which was theirs, a valued possession which had special meaning.

There are several types of loss. The most traumatic loss is that of a significant person (that is, with whom the person had an important relationship, one which held special meaning) through death, separation, divorce or distance. Another type of loss arises from a change in a significant relationship.

Grief can also result from loss of a pet – through disappearance, separation or death and the loss of objects due to burglary or fire. Objects can be replaced but the feelings attached to them can't be. Objects have sentimental value because they are associated with a particular moment in time. People can experience loss when they move house, too – the loss of leaving a place which is familiar and the scene of special memories.

People grieve if they lose part of their body, such as a limb, an organ or their sight. The image people have of themselves is linked with their appearance and the way the world sees them. They connect their attractiveness with the measure of their worth and how lovable they are. Any loss of function can lead to a loss of their roles as, for example, wage earner; father or mother; wife or husband.

Another kind of loss is that associated with human development and life s milestones. This can include the loss of opportunity to be a mother or, in elderly people, loss of strength or physical wellbeing.

Previous experiences of loss may provide people with the ability to cope with a new loss. This means that what is a loss to one person may not be a loss to another. Emotional and physical wellbeing also give people greater resources to handle losses. Care workers meet people who have limited emotional and physical resources for handling their loss. Misuse of alcohol or drugs, and the inability to rest or sleep, all interfere with what is regarded as the 'normal' grieving process. Family attitudes to loss, and different cultural, ethnic and religious backgrounds, also influence the way people deal with loss or death.

This book looks at all areas of loss and grief. It does not deal only with loss through death, although most people view this as the most significant loss. Care workers also spend a lot of time helping clients come to terms with other losses.

A person's inability to control loss causes feelings of helplessness and despair. Care workers have no control over these feelings in their clients, but they may increase their chances of encountering them if they are negligent or unable to see the warning signs.

Philosophers and scientists have attempted to understand and even control death. The fact that everyone must face his own death as well as the death of others not only creates anxiety but also gives meaning to life. The thoughts a person has about death affect the way he lives. These thoughts can make him feel threatened, give him pain, or inspire him and give deeper meaning to a relationship because he values the attachment.

It is essential that you, as a care worker, examine your own thoughts and feelings on these difficult issues in order to help others cope with them. This book confronts you with some of the more painful and difficult areas of life. If you are to be an effective care worker it is important that you face up to these uncomfortable thoughts.

We can explore these life issues positively if we make use of both our personal life experiences and the example of others. This book also explores various ideas and theories, and looks at what has been learned over the years about the processes which people go through to help them come to terms with the pain of loss.

Loss, separation, dying and death are very personal, individual experiences. This book offers some guidelines for sharing with, understanding, and caring for, people who are encountering these experiences. As a care worker, you may feel as if you are intruding into someone's most private moments, but the very nature of your work means it is almost impossible to avoid such intimacy. The understanding you gain from working through the issues of loss and grief will help you to value and respect individual needs and beliefs, as well as give you an insight into what you can actually do to help.

To the reader

Here are some questions which may occur to you before you start to read this book

Who is this book for?

Anyone involved in caring. It has been designed with you – the reader – in mind. We've tried to make it look and feel friendly and attractive.

Do I need to enrol in a course to use this book?

Certainly not, although you may find that it is used by many caring courses. You can use it on your own, at your workplace as part of an assessment programme, if you're in employment, or as part of a more formal training programme at a college or other institution.

Where can I read this book?

Anywhere you like. You can read it in 'snatches', if this is more convenient for you, or you can interrupt your reading to do some of the exercises. It may help you to write on it, if it's your own copy. As you will see, the book has been designed to be used in a very flexible way.

Are there any special features that I should be aware of before starting to read this book?

You'll find it a great help to know the following:

Definitions

Sometimes a key word might be unfamiliar to some readers, or we might want to be sure that the precise meaning is clear. We have tried to pick out such words and give their meaning at the place where the word is first mentioned. The word and its definition have been set off in the margin.

Examples

There's no substitute for a good example to make a point or convey a message. We've included as many examples as possible and have set these off from the main text with boxes, so that you can skip them if you like, or locate them again if you found them particularly helpful.

Exercises

These have been set off from the text in boxes and in a different typeface. The exercises can extend your knowledge considerably and reinforce what you've read in the main text. You can do the exercises on your own, with a group, or under the direction of a tutor. Or you can choose not to do them at all, or to do them later, after you've read and absorbed the text. The choice is yours.

Remember: this is *your* book – enjoy it!

ABOUT TERMINOLOGY

Throughout the text the recipients of all types of care are referred to as 'clients' and those involved in providing the care as 'care workers'. For simplicity, clients are always referred to as 'he' and care workers as 'she'.

1 Separation and loss

This chapter considers some life changes and how they produce feelings of separation and loss in each of us. Many of the developments in our lives, and the changes they produce, are not under our control. For example, we have no control over the first sudden change we experience – leaving the safety and comfort of the womb and finding ourselves out in the big wide world! On other occasions we do control the change, perhaps by making the decision to stop working in one area and move to another.

EARLY MESSAGES

In his book, *Sadness and Depression*, John Bowlby describes what he observed when he studied attachment and loss. He described how we make powerful bonds of affection with our primary care giver, usually our mother. The bond is fundamental to our feelings of wellbeing and safety. If it is broken or threatened we feel acute anxiety. This anxiety can be described as grief.

From an early age we have to cope with fears of loss or separation. Both a young child and his parents have to cope with attachment and separation. Some early memories of these separations may remain with us. Can you remember:

- being left with a friend or relative for the first time, when you were under 5 years old

- suddenly feeling lost, perhaps on a crowded beach or in a big department store

- going to nursery or school for the first time

- staying with friends or relatives for a prolonged period of time, while one parent or both parents were in hospital or on holiday?

See exercise 1

> ### EXERCISE I
>
> Write a short account of how you felt at a time of separation from a member or members of your family.
> How did your behaviour reveal the distress you felt?

"anxiety"
a state or feeling of unease, uncertainty or fear, resulting from an anticipated threat or danger

Children express very strong feelings about loss, often reacting with opposite extremes of behaviour. These can range from sadness, stillness and a quiet withdrawn response, to loud expressions of fear and anxiety. Parents find these extremes difficult to cope with and often label the child's response 'bad behaviour' without looking for the cause.

During our early years we are given some powerful messages from our families about the expression of feelings associated with loss. For example, a child loses a toy and screams and cries for it. A parent may tell the child to be quiet, that losing a toy does not matter much and he is 'soft' to cry about it. These messages tell the child that his reactions to the loss are a sign of weakness. Many children grow up without ever being allowed to give expression to their feelings of loss.

However, if parents are able to understand how much the child valued the lost object, then they will recognise and allow his need to express his distress.

As children we receive messages that either allow us to express our loss, and share our feelings about it, or that teach us to deny how we feel. Sexual stereotyping is also introduced into these messages. Little girls are allowed to express their feelings but not little boys. Boys are told:

> *'Big boys don't cry'*

> *'Don't let other boys see you crying'*

> *'People will say you are soft'*

Many people can cope with the tears and distress of a woman but find the same behaviour unacceptable in a man. Messages given in childhood may make men suppress their feelings of loss and grief. If men continually push these feelings deep down inside themselves instead of expressing them they can face serious difficulties later in life.

LIFE CHANGES

Some life changes produce feelings of loss which lead to grief. Many life changes produce gains as well as losses, but we may have been taught from childhood to concentrate on the gains and to deny any distressing feelings.

People either handle life's developmental changes easily or find that a particular change or milestone causes difficulties. Also, not everyone encounters the same milestones. Figure 1 gives a list of life's milestones.

Figure 1
Life's milestones

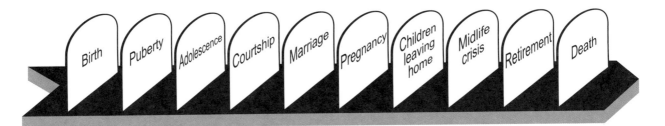

Many milestones produce more feelings of loss than others, depending on the circumstances. For example, pregnancy should produce joy, but it can be seen as a sign of the loss of childhood innocence if it occurs at adolescence. The individual may grieve for the lost fun that adolescence could have brought but which is now denied.

A life change involving a sense of loss may only happen once. If people manage to deal with their feelings of loss they can move on. If they fail to acknowledge the loss involved in the event then when they face the same sort of event again they may have to grieve for both events.

To understand what this means, think about two events which can involve feelings of loss as well as gain – marriage and moving house. If either of these events occur for a second time, when the gains and losses of the first time have not been dealt with, then the feelings from the first event become mixed up with those from the second.

See Exercise 2.

EXERCISE 2

Head one half your paper 'Gains' and the other 'Losses'.

List gains in marriage in one column and the losses in the other.

Then do the same for moving house.

INFANCY AND CHILDHOOD

The effects of separation on infants and children are now well known and this has resulted in, for example, hospitals providing longer visiting times or open access for close family members. Open access reduces the feelings of alarm experienced by children and young people when they have to spend time in hospital. However, some institutions cannot allow open access. When children or young people are taken into care, and access is denied or closely supervised, their feelings of fear and anxiety are more apparent. They may fear further loss and outbursts of distress can occur.

Children who are in hospital or residential care without their mothers often become withdrawn and communicate less and less with care givers. Their agitation and anger may be directed towards the parent substitute, the care giver. We all need to protest about our losses; if children behave badly when their parents reappear they are protesting about the anxiety they have had to go through.

Bowlby describes three phases which children pass through when they are in hospital or residential care:

- protest
- despair
- detachment.

The signs of these phases are clues which help all those involved with care of the children to work with their feelings.

ADOLESCENCE

Adolescence covers a wide range so we cannot say people have reached this milestone in life simply because of their age. Some 12-year-old girls show as much adolescent behaviour as 18-year-old boys. For example, girls feel embarrassed about their bodies and may be reluctant to undress in front of others.

If, as a care worker, you are talking to a young person on his own because he does not want his parents to be there, you may face some hostility from the parents. The parents may feel the young person is still a child and may be worried about losing him. You may be trying to acknowledge the adult in the young person and his emergence as a separate person from his parents. The parents may also be hurt because their child has confided in you and not in them – another painful reminder of the loss of the dependent child. In part, the parents value the fact that their child is becoming an adult, but another part of them experiences a feeling of loss.

A teenager's feeling of sexuality, and his insights into an adult world, produce in parents a powerful feeling of something which is gone, never to return. Adults often describe this change as a 'loss of innocence', when children's involvement with the world of make-believe or fairy tales comes to an end. This comes home to many parents when their children stop believing in Father Christmas.

For the young person experiencing it the shift towards adolescence, and its associated sexual changes, produces fears about loss. Some find that their awakened sexual feelings prevent them from expressing intimate feelings towards their parents because intimacy is now associated with sexual activity. This results in a distancing from parents, with the accompanying feelings of loss. These changes are a reminder that the adolescent is moving away from childhood towards the eventual loss of parental protection.

The parents also feel the loss if the young adult's beliefs and values change from those he was brought up with. They express this grief in phrases like:

'He does not listen to us any more'

'We are growing apart'

The adolescent, in turn, feels isolated from his parents. The fear of further conflict may make it seem as if they are growing apart. He expresses his feelings of loss and the cause of his grief in phrases like:

'They do not understand me'

'It doesn't matter what I do, they find fault'

Sometimes, the crisis in the relationship ends in the young person moving out of the family home – another painful loss.

MARRIAGE

Many people spend a major part of their adult lives as a husband or wife. For some, the marriage ceremony is seen as a necessary condition to living together and sexual activity. However, cohabiting is now commonplace and this too requires commitment from both partners, with the same feelings of loss as those experienced in a marriage breakdown if the relationship does not work out.

Try exercise 3

EXERCISE 3

Many people take on traditional roles within a marriage. Copy the following lists of traditional roles onto separate sheets of paper headed 'Male' and 'Female':

MALE	FEMALE
Strong	Housekeeper
Wage earner	Loyal
Head of the house	Attractive
Arranges social interaction	Supportive
Active sexual partner	Cook
Decision-maker	Manager
Authoritarian	Uninformed
	Submissive
	Sacrificial
	Passive sexual partner

Imagine that the man loses three of his traditional male roles, for example, if he is made redundant, or has to stay off work for several months because of illness. How might the effect of these losses be shown in him as a person, for example, in his feelings, attitudes and behaviour? Do the same for the woman losing three traditional female roles, perhaps through promotion at her work or through the demands of looking after an elderly relative.

MIDLIFE CRISIS

A lot of jokes are made about midlife crisis, but it can be a very real experience. It is hard to pinpoint 'midlife' to a particular age; some people associate it with the menopause in women

"menopause"
the end of the period of possible sexual reproduction, shown when menstrual periods stop, usually between the ages of 45 and 50

Other people connect midlife crisis with a time of reassessment of a person's life and the direction it is taking. For many people this reassessment occurs spontaneously, without them making a conscious decision about it. Sometimes it happens when people are in a hospital or institutional care. The change of pace they experience allows them more time to think, especially if they cannot sleep in the middle of the night.

A midlife crisis may occur because a person has arrived at a particular point in his life – perhaps in his job or in his relationship – and wants to look at the best way for using his resources from his new position. He may feel a sense of sadness and loss at not having reached his goals at this stage in his life.

On the other hand, he may have reached his peak of achievement and will now have to gradually reduce his activities. He could put all his energies and attention into new and stimulating areas of activity. This is an exciting idea but it may produce feelings of fear and panic because failure in this new direction will, in turn, result in sadness and loss.

During this period friends and relatives may die. People become more aware that they too will die some day and they show feelings of grief. They may say things like:

'I can't keep up with things any more'

'I will have to learn to slow down'

'I must remember that I am not as young as I used to be'

This confirms that they feel they are on what could be called 'the downward slope' of life and must take things easy. Some people can cope with this and are pleased with the signs that they can begin to opt out of a more competitive world. Others express feelings of regret and loss at leaving this phase of their lives. Their reaction is more extreme – a feeling of doom because they see this as 'the beginning of the end.'

RETIREMENT AND REDUNDANCY

Some people welcome retirement; they plan what they will do and take courses to develop new hobbies. Other people find the effects of retirement or redundancy devastating. Partners have to spend longer periods together and this makes some people feel as if they have lost their freedom, autonomy and financial status.

People's occupations give them status. They may find the loss of that status difficult to handle emotionally and it can take some time for an adjustment to take place.

DIVORCE AND SEPARATION

An increasing number of people end their marriages by divorcing. This is not only painful for the individuals directly involved, but other people are also affected by friends and relatives who go through the divorce process. Some people say they have emerged from their divorce feeling more fulfilled and having gained from the experience. But for most it is a time full of sadness, pain and significant loss.

As more people divorce the social stigma attached is reduced. However, many divorcees feel that breaking their marriage vows alienates them from their church and the shared beliefs of others in their religion; for them this is a major loss. Divorced and separated people also find that people they know often avoid talking about what has happened, in the same way as they might avoid discussing and confronting death. People may cross to the other side of the road so they do not have to meet a bereaved friend and acknowledge a death and its difficulties, they will do the same to avoid awkward meetings with a person who is divorced or separated.

Most people know about the embarrassment they feel trying to find the right words to say to someone who has experienced a significant loss. This makes an already difficult situation more uncomfortable for the person involved. For example, children feel different because they only have one parent at the school open night; women who are in hospital after having a baby sense everyone's discomfort if the father doesn't come at visiting time. People in these situations feel abandoned as well as a terrible sense of loss. Loss in these situations produces stigma.

"autonomy"
a feeling of independence or personal freedom; being able to make your own decisions

"stigma"
a mark of shame or disgrace

6

Our situation in life – married, single, employed – gives us status. It indicates our position in society and how we are recognised and valued by others. This may explain why people ask the following questions when they first meet someone – it is a sign of their need to fit an individual into a wider group of people:

> *'What does he do?'*
>
> *'Is she married?'*
>
> *'Where do they live?'*
>
> *'Do you know his parents?'*
>
> *'Does she have any children?'*

The outer, public part of our lives consists of the position we have in society, our family, our social class and our work. This is how we present ourselves to the outside world. The loss of any part of the outer picture has a profound effect on the way people see us and on how we feel about ourselves inside. Our feelings and our reactions to any situation make up the inner, private part of our lives.

BEING A CLIENT

Losses occur when an individual becomes a client. The illness, injury or condition that has affected the person will result in loss of image: a feeling that he has lost the person he was. (This is considered in more detail in Chapter 3.) If the person goes to live in a hospital, or some other form of residential care, there is a loss of home and community; he may also have to move from the neighbourhood where his family lives. These losses are easy to see and understand, but the loss of self-esteem is not so easily understood.

"self-esteem"
judgement or evaluation of your worth in relation to your ideal self and to the performance of others

A client who needs care from a care worker in his own home will also experience feelings of loss. A person who loses control over his ability to care for himself can have feelings of grief. For him, becoming a client is seen as a threat both physically and emotionally. The client worries that he may come to some harm and have no control over what happens to him.

REVIEW

All of life's changes – not just the milestones described in this chapter – have the potential to result in loss, with its accompanying sadness and distress, as well as gain. The following list shows some of the life changes people experience, listed according to the degree of difficulty involved in coping with them.

It is important that we are aware of the losses involved in change as well as the advantages. If we fail to acknowledge the losses at the time they occur then they may re-emerge and make the effects of a subsequent loss more difficult than they should be. This results in the misery of one loss piling onto the unresolved misery of a previous loss.

SUMMARY EXERCISE

Look again at the explanation of self-esteem on page 7.
Make some notes about your own ideal self.

Your ideal self is the way you would like to be and how you would like others to see you.

- In what way do you not match up to this?

- How do you manage to deal with this loss of your ideal self?

LIFE CHANGES IN ORDER OF DIFFICULTY

- Death of spouse
- Divorce
- Marital separation
- Prison sentence
- Death of a close family member
- Major personal injury or illness
- Marriage
- Loss of job or redundancy
- Marital reconciliation
- Retirement
- Major change in the health or behaviour of a family member
- Pregnancy
- Sexual difficulties
- Gaining a new family member for example through birth, adoption or an older person moving in
- Major business readjustment, for example a merger, reorganisation or bankruptcy
- Major change in financial state either a lot worse off or a lot better off than before
- Death of a close friend
- Change of job
- Major change in the number of arguments with spouse, either a lot more or a lot less than usual, about subjects like childbearing and personal habits
- Taking out a mortgage or loan for a major purpose, for example, for a home or a business
- Foreclosure on a mortgage or loan
- Major change in responsibilities at work such as promotion or demotion
- Son or daughter leaving home, for example, to marry or attend college
- Trouble with in-laws
- Outstanding personal achievement

2 Grief

"bereavement"
the fact of being bereaved, that is, deprived by death of a relative, friend or loved one

Grief describes the reactions a person experiences while in a state of bereavement.

These reactions can include physical complaints and illnesses, as well as emotional responses, such as anger and guilt. The intensity of the reactions varies depending on the type of loss, the circumstances of the death, and the strength of the person's attachment to the deceased. Normal grieving is the process by which a person adapts to a significant loss, that is, the loss of someone or something meaningful and valued which he possessed personally. Death of a significant person is one of the most difficult losses to deal with, but grief can also result from the loss of a pet through death, loss or separation.

Grieving may also occur after the loss of a material object that a person particularly valued. The object may have had a special meaning because it was given to the person by a relative or friend. For example, you may have a piece of jewellery which commemorates a significant moment in your life or which is an expression of some powerful feelings associated with another person. Some possessions symbolise special moments for us and bring back particular memories or periods in our lives. How we feel and behave when we discover the loss of something we value reflects some of the difficulties we also have in dealing with death.

Think about this by trying Exercise 5.

EXERCISE 5

This exercise will help you work out how you felt when you discovered the loss of an object you valued (*not* a person or a living thing, such as a pet).

You need 2 sheets of paper; head one '**Feelings**' and the other '**Behaviour**'. Under 'Feelings' make a list of words that describe your feelings on discovering the loss of the object. Under 'Behaviour' make a list of the words that describe how you set about finding it.

Pay particular attention to how you looked for the object and what happened.

In completing Exercise 5 you probably found that you were able to cope with some of your feelings better than others. The way you responded to the loss of an object reflects how you might respond to the death of a person because these responses are part of the normal process of grieving.

Grief is often thought of as a negative experience, but in fact it is the process by which people are healed and which helps them to emerge from a significant loss. Because people have difficulty in recognising the value of grief they attempt to avoid the process altogether; other people join with them by helping them to avoid the pain of grief. Understanding the value of grief, and helping people through it, is more useful to them in the long term. Grief aids a person's recovery from the death of a significant loved one.

This chapter looks at the process of grief, at the stages and difficulties involved, and at the kind of grief from which it is hard to emerge. It will help you gain an insight into the value of the grieving process and what your role as a care worker can be in helping people through it.

THEORIES ABOUT GRIEF

FREUD

Sigmund Freud wrote a paper called *Mourning and Melancholia* (1917) in which he described the work of mourning. His study shows the differences between normal grief and depression, and describes what happens when a person reaches a depression (or melancholia) beyond the normal symptoms of grief. Freud felt that grief should not be regarded as an unhealthy condition which needed treatment. It is interesting to compare his point of view with the one held in the 1990s, when many grieving people are referred to their GP for treatment of their symptoms.

Freud described mourning and depression as being similar but different. The difference is that a person suffering from depression shows an obvious lowering of self-esteem and also shows self-reproach to a masochistic (that is, self-damaging) degree. Freud describes how, in normal mourning, the person has no powerful, ambivalent feelings (that is, no strong feelings of love and hate) or other powerful opposites. It is the ambivalent feelings which lead the person to show the obsessive self-reproachment – he feels hurt, neglected and wounded, resulting in the false belief that he is going to be punished. In normal grief none of this occurs.

"ambivalent"
to have conflicting feelings or attitudes towards a person or object

LINDEMANN

The first major theorist to study grieving was Eric Lindemann. He described the person's first responses as shock, disbelief and an inability to accept the death. Denial of the loss produces bodily symptoms, such as tightness in the throat, choking sensations, shortness of breath, weak muscles, sighing and exhaustion.

As the person begins to accept the loss the working phase of normal grieving begins. The person may be disinterested in daily affairs and feel anger, hostility, irritability and guilt. He may blame himself for being negligent and have feelings of loss and loneliness. At the same time, the person often distances himself from others and feels a strong desire to be alone. He also experiences feelings of unreality, insomnia, loss of appetite and restlessness. He may want to talk a lot and to be active all the time, even if the activity does not have much purpose. Yet the person may also be apathetic (lacking interest in anything) and be unable to take part in organised activities.

According to Lindemann, the grieving person then frees himself from emotional bonds and adjusts to life without the loved one. In the final stages of grieving he establishes new interests and relationships, gradually re-entering an active lifestyle in which his energy is no longer focused on the loss.

BOWLBY

John Bowlby described the loss of self (or part of self) and the loss of objects in three phases:

- protest
- disorganisation
- restructuring.

Protest

The first phase, protest, is characterised by feelings of anger, disbelief, shock and yearning (great longing). The person focuses on thoughts of loss by crying, searching consciously (or unconsciously) to recover the loss and by making appeals for help. Sleep, digestion and appetite may be disturbed during this stage.

Disorganisation

This stage is shown by despair, depression, withdrawal, social isolation and a slowing down of physical activities. There may also be obvious signs of regression, that is, a return to an earlier, more primitive form of behaviour.

Restructuring

In the third phase the person breaks away from the attachment, developing new interests and attachments. He returns to a level of functioning similar to that experienced before the loss.

Bowlby's theory is very task-orientated, that is, the phases he described are demonstrated by the things people are involved in at the various stages of grief. For example, in the first phase people wander around looking for the lost one or for signs that he may still be available; in the third phase people learn new skills. Bowlby suggested that we can recognise which phase a person is going through by looking at the purpose of the tasks they are carrying out.

PARKES

"stress"
emotional pressure caused by difficulties in life (a stressor is a situation or stimulus which causes stress)

Colin Murray Parkes described grief as a major stressor which can greatly affect a person's health. In his research, Parkes found:

> 'every indication that the grieving person is in a state of high arousal during much of the time, and occasionally approaches panic.'

The loss threatens the security of the individual and places him in a state of alarm. This state of alarm is a characteristic response for the survivor to make when the death of a significant person first occurs,

Parkes believed that the reasons for grief were resistance to change and a reluctance to give up possessions, people, status and expectations. He outlined four stages which occur during the grieving process:

- numbness
- searching and pining
- depression
- recovery

Numbness

The first stage, numbness, forms a psychological and physical barrier which blocks out pain. This barrier of mind and body allows the grieving person to carry on with the normal activities of everyday life.

Searching and pining

During the second stage, searching and pining, the bereaved person is unable to concentrate on anything other than the death and the person who has died. Pining is the emotional response to this searching for the person and results in what Parkes called 'pangs of grief'.

Depression

The third stage, depression, is the time when the person admits that searching is pointless and his intense pangs of grief subside. His anger also loses its strength and is replaced by feelings of apathy and despair. During this stage the grieving person is forced to accept that he will have to make changes in order to survive.

Recovery

In the recovery stage old ways of thinking are left behind. This releases the individual from the past and allows him to begin living again.

All the theories described in this chapter describe stages of grieving. If you are able to recognise where people are in the grief process you will be able to make contact with them and talk to them more meaningfully.

See Exercise 6.

EXERCISE 6

Look again at the theories we have discussed.

What do all the theories have in common and what are the differences between them?

(Reference sources are listed on page 58)

DETERMINANTS OF GRIEF

From his studies on grief Parkes found that certain facts connected with death affected the outcome of the grieving process. He called these facts determinants of grief because they can be used to predict difficulties which might occur as the person works through his grief. The determinants of grief are:

- mode of death
- nature of the attachment
- who the person was?
- historical antecedents
- personality variables
- social variables.

Try Exercise 7 before continuing.

EXERCISE 7

Sometimes texts describing the grief process use the phrase 'resolution of grief'.

Jot down your thoughts on the question, 'Is grief ever resolved?'

Most people who have worked with grieving people describe the process of grief as 'coming to the end'. In other words, they feel that rather than saying the grief is resolved the person works – or struggles – towards living with the loss. People often describe the grieving process as 'work' because they feel that dealing with their grief is a job they have to do – they have no choice if they are to survive. Although each of the determinants of grief highlights possible difficulties in the grieving process, it is important to remember that bereaved people need to experience the process of grief if they are to emerge from their loss. The next part of this chapter looks at each of the determinants of grief in more detail.

MODE OF DEATH

'Mode of death' means how the death occurred. A death from natural causes like illness, even if it is sudden, usually causes fewer problems than a traumatic death which involved injuries that damaged the body. Most people want to know whether the deceased person suffered or if he knew anything about the process of dying. Some people think it is unhealthy to dwell on these things, but bereaved people need to spend time on this part of their grief. Death caused by a road traffic accident, or an accident at home or at work, can arouse stronger feelings of anger about its injustice than a death from natural causes. People may discuss at length the verdict of the Coroner's court (in England and Wales) or the Fatal Accident Enquiry (in Scotland), concentrating on the fact that no one knows all the facts about the death. If vital information is missing it may be impossible to find out exactly what happened. Often, people can find someone or something to blame for the death – an individual, the organisation which employed the person, society, God. But it is difficult to find any relief in making accusations if the deceased person was to blame because it is not easy to

13

talk negatively or angrily about someone who is dead. The place where the death occurred is an important part of the mode of death. For example, was the deceased at home or in a strange place? The pain is greater for bereaved people if the deceased person was far away from home when he died, or with a stranger, and it is even worse if he was alone.

THE NATURE OF THE ATTACHMENT

The strengths and weaknesses of an attachment between two people become very clear after one of them dies. The strengths of the relationship, what its loss represents and the security gained from it, will dominate the thoughts and feelings of a bereaved person. He will also find that he holds ambivalent feelings towards the deceased.

It is very difficult to cope with these opposing, powerful feelings. We all know how it is possible to love and hate someone at the same time; after bereavement many people find these contrasting feelings almost unbearable.

WHO WAS THE PERSON WAS

'Who was the person?' may seem like an obvious question to ask, but it is important to have some idea of who the deceased was in relation to the bereaved person. During the grieving process the bereaved person re-evaluates his relationships. The position of the deceased in the structure of the family cannot be taken as a clear indication of the enormity of loss the person will feel. It is not helpful to make assumptions about whether or not people were close by their 'official' relationship.

HISTORICAL ANTECEDENTS

'Historical antecedants' describes what the bereaved person's previous experience of death has been. Have past contacts with death or other life crises had a good outcome or one of pain and suffering? If the person has failed to confront loss in the past it may re-emerge, making present problems worse because it is difficult for the sufferer to work out the source of his pain and anguish. This can become a serious problem for a bereaved person; he may need some counselling to understand his problems and make them more manageable.

Other recent life changes, or recent depressive illness, can increase the difficulty the person has in handling the loss. If he has channelled a lot of energy and resources into tackling these challenges he will be left without any reserves to deal with another emotionally demanding situation.

PERSONALITY VARIABLES

People who feel they have some control over their lives, and who see life as a challenge, are the ones most likely to recover from grief. The personality characteristics of people who have dependent, ambivalent relationships make it more difficult for them to work successfully through grief. Earlier personal experience of grief, especially childhood loss of a parent or parents, makes a person more vulnerable. It is not easy to reduce the effects of childhood loss.

SOCIAL VARIABLES

Some deaths alienate and isolate people; others produce gains for them. The gain may be the freedom to leave a group or community, or to escape from restrictions produced by a relationship. However, if the one left behind always felt like an extension of the other person this causes particular problems. For example, many social engagements attended by a boss's wife centre around her husband's role. In some cultures and religions it is customary for bereaved people to be looked after and showered with offers of help; this does not always happen in Western society, where people may be left to cope alone. Determinants of grief can be used to identify areas which may have a strongly negative effect on the bereaved person and make his grief less easy to manage.

Use this information when you try Exercise 7.

EXERCISE 7

Read the following example carefully.

A young wife lived on an army base in Germany where her husband was stationed.

They had 2 children aged 14 and 7.

When the husband was killed in a road accident the wife and children had to return to Britain to live, temporarily, with her parents.

Which of the determinants of grief would have a major effect on the young wife? Use them to describe her losses and difficulties.

EMERGING FROM A DIFFICULT DEATH

Some types of death are more likely to cause long-term physical and psychological problems than others. The circumstances of these deaths, particularly some baby and child deaths can result in lasting emotional damage for the people involved. It is important, therefore, to identify any individuals who are at risk and guide them to the appropriate support agency. Deaths, which produce greater than average difficulties in grieving, are:

- stillbirth
- Sudde Infant Death Syndrome (SIDS)
- death by trauma or in a disaster
- suicide
- sudden death.

There is also more likely to be a breakdown in relationships amongst the people left behind after a death in these circumstances.

STILLBIRTH

If a baby is stillborn then the hopes built up during months of pregnancy are suddenly gone. It is not only the mother who is affected; fathers also develop an attachment to the baby before it is born and may be present at the birth.

Some stillbirths occur with foreknowledge of the event and it is known that the baby is already dead. This is very painful for parents, especially if they have to wait for the natural onset of labour to produce a dead baby. In these cases, some anticipatory grieving may take place when the intrauterine death has been diagnosed (that is, death in the womb). Anticipatory grieving means grieving before the loss takes place; it is discussed in more detail on page 31. Sometimes the news of the death confirms the knowledge that the baby had a congenital abnormality. The parents, or mother, then have to cope with the way the baby looks, something which they had only been able to imagine during the pregnancy.

A mother may sense that something is wrong during her pregnancy, perhaps because of strange sensations or a lack of movement. At first, she may keep her fears to herself in the hope that they are unfounded. A mother may only begin to confront the loss when she finally shares her worries with her partner.

When a stillbirth is expected there is a quiet atmosphere in the labour room, not the usual feeling of excitement. In the past, the baby was removed quickly, but nowadays the mother is given time to hold and look at her baby. Most parents are prepared for the worst and usually find that, even if their baby is deformed, the reality is not as upsetting as they had feared. If a stillbirth is not expected there may be frantic efforts to resuscitate the baby while the parents hope against all odds for success. They then have to face the awful news that all efforts have failed.

If their baby is stillborn parents want to find out whether more could have been done to save him. They want to ask a lot of questions about why the baby died:

> *Had they done anything to harm their unborn child?*
>
> *Had there been any other congenital abnormalities in the family?*
>
> *If so, whose side was the abnormality on and which parent carries the gene responsible?*

Parents who are prevented from seeing their dead baby face added difficulties in dealing with the death and their grief. Many hospitals take photographs in case a parent who refused to look at a dead baby changes his mind and wants to look later.

In her book, *The Anatomy of a Bereavement*, Beverley Raphael describes how her work and that of others has revealed the value of this contact with the dead baby. Parents need to be reassured that any stories they have heard about stillborn babies being disposed of in the hospital incinerator are entirely untrue. It is important that they know they can give their baby a name, and a proper service and burial. Talking about a funeral recognises that the baby was a person. To his mother and father the baby had become a special person despite the fact that he did not live after birth. The parents need to acknowledge that they had hopes and plans for him. Some fathers want to protect their partners from the pain of death and try and prevent them from seeing the dead baby. The value of this contact with the baby should be explained carefully and sensitively to them.

It is not helpful to say to the mother or father at the time of their loss, 'You can always have another baby.' They may react angrily to remarks like this. Some parents will find that their grief is eased by another pregnancy, but others may feel they do not want to have another baby if they think the risks are too great. Marital and sexual difficulties are common after a stillbirth so counselling may be needed. If the mother was heavily sedated during and after the birth the risk of a poor outcome in dealing with the grief is increased. On the anniversary of the event people will react in the same way as they do to the anniversary of any death.

It is important that the parents can talk to a good listener and tell them about the whole ordeal in detail. They need someone who can listen to all the details without wanting to avoid any of the pain they feel. The counselling may include discussion of ideas expressed in phrases like:

> *'There must be something wrong with someone who produces a deformed, dead baby.'*

> *'We must have done something wicked for this to happen to us and our baby'.*

Family and friends are often unsure about how to respond to the unexpected outcome of the pregnancy. Parents may feel hurt because people do not acknowledge what has happened to their baby. Although the outcome of the pregnancy was not what was hoped for it should still be acknowledged; people need to know that their family and friends care about what has happened.

SUDDEN INFANT DEATH SYNDROME (SIDS)

In the United Kingdom, Sudden Infant Death Syndrome (SIDS) is often referred to as a 'cot death'. SIDS occurs when an apparently healthy baby is put to sleep in a cot or pram as normal but found to be dead the next time someone goes to look at him. The baby may have had a minor symptom, such as a snuffly nose, or may not have taken his feed as he normally would. SIDS is also more common in boys than girls and is more frequent in the winter months.

One out of every 500 babies born alive in the United Kingdom dies suddenly and unexpectedly; in the absence of a known cause of death these deaths are registered as SIDS. Sometimes vomit is found around the baby's mouth or on the pillow so that it seems as if the baby choked. However, SIDS babies do not die from asphyxiation (choking). Babies found face down may appear to have suffocated, but SIDS is not caused by external suffocation.

The parents will want to know why their baby has died. They may believe they have done something wrong, or neglected the baby in some way, and that there must be an explanation for the death of a normal baby. Parents spend hours asking questions aloud to themselves. They are desperate for answers but there aren't any. They will repeat the same questions over and over again and, as a care worker, you must give them the same attention each time.

It is important for people to see and hold the baby after it is found and also before the funeral.

Care workers may have the difficult role of accompanying parents and relatives who sit and hold their babies. Parents need to be allowed to express anger at other people's questions and responses, too. It is insensitive for people to say at the time of death, 'You can always have another baby' and it does not give the parents space to grieve the loss of the baby who has just died. When a death is unexpected a uniformed policeman, a representative of the Coroner's Office or, in Scotland, the Procurator Fiscal's Department, may have to ask many questions. The parents and family may feel they are being accused of something. Everyone should understand why those searching questions have to be asked. When a baby or young person dies everyone close to him feels sad about the individual who is lost, but they also wonder, 'What might he have been? What might he have given to the world?'

Think about this further by trying Exercise 8.

EXERCISE 8

Make a list of things parents are denied for the future when they lose a child. This will give you a greater insight into how the death affects them. The list might begin:

      Watching him or her grow

      Being grandparents

DEATH BY TRAUMA OR DISASTER

Another kind of death which people find difficult to deal with is one which damages the body because of a sudden, unexpected event. There are always a lot of questions surrounding such events, particularly the question,

    'Who is to blame?'

Accidents and disasters vary in nature and severity. For example, fires, murders and traffic accidents occur more frequently than tornadoes, earthquakes and floods. Most of these events are beyond anyone's control yet the psychological problems resulting from them produce strong feelings of hostility towards governments and other authorities. Studies of the behaviour of the family and friends of people killed in sudden disastrous events have identified three phases of response:

- the period of impact
- the recoil period
- the post-traumatic period.

The period of impact

At this stage people's behaviour is disorganised and they are less likely to respond to directions. The panic shown in disaster films does not happen very often in real life. People are either stunned by the deaths which have occurred or appear outwardly cool and collected. They often talk of a lack of feeling or emotion and behave as if they have no mind or will to make decisions. A small group of people will scream and cry, or will become confused and paralysed by the event. Feelings of hopelessness, agitation and disorganisation are common during the impact phase.

The recoil period

During this period the stresses of the impact phase have ceased; some individuals escape them altogether. People gradually become aware of what has happened and their ability to express emotions returns. Victims need to be with other people, to express their feelings and, usually, their sense of gratitude for the help they have received. After a disaster, people who have been bereaved or injured may try to play down the importance of their loss or pain and ask that others are helped first. Some people feel guilty simply because they have survived. During this period they seem to be more open to suggestion and more accessible. There are signs that others can start to make meaningful contact with them.

The post-traumatic period

This can be the longest phase of response. For some people the emotional crisis occurs six months after the disaster took place. At the start of the post-traumatic stage morale improves and people show a sense of identity with the community. For example, they become involved in plans to make sure that something positive results from the disastrous event. They may devote their energies to erecting a memorial to mark the occasion or set up a fund which will help the whole community. Dreams and nightmares may occur at this stage as the victims of traumatic events realise exactly what the disaster meant for themselves and others in terms of loss or bereavement.

SUICIDE

Television programmes and films often show a person committing suicide by doing something dramatic, like jumping from a high building. In fact, most people who commit suicide do so quietly – the most common method involves swallowing tablets, often with large amounts of alcohol.

"psychiatry"
the study and treatment of diseases of the mind

When a person commits suicide other people may wonder if he had been suffering from a psychiatric illness. This question may be difficult to answer because many people who take their own lives have not had a psychiatric evaluation. People who have a history of psychiatric illness are more at risk, but if no further information is available the person may be described as having killed himself 'while the balance of his mind was disturbed'. This mayor may not mean he was mentally ill. Less than half the people who attempt suicide are diagnosed as being mentally ill; most are going through a life crisis associated with losing, or the threat of losing, a relationship.

It is also difficult to say whether or not suicide is a rational act. People who believe suicide can be a reasonable choice for someone to make under certain conditions will argue that suicide can be a rational act. People who would never consider suicide under any circumstances will always label it as an irrational act.

In the same way, people make a subjective (that is, personal) response to the events that caused the person to take his own life. For example, you may think that if you were in severe pain from terminal cancer committing suicide would be a rational choice for you to make in order to end your suffering. But would you set fire to yourself in public to draw attention to an issue and bring about social change? Yet both these acts have the same outcome because they are both acts of suicide. In the end, each person must make his own decision about what is or isn't rational.

It is widely believed that people who threaten suicide, or who make repeated, half-hearted attempts, are not suicidal but are seeking attention. Their family and friends, and the workers caring for them, may feel angry towards them. They are often accused of wasting time and trying to manipulate people.

However, the fact is that people who show suicidal behaviour are serious suicidal risks. If a person is contemplating suicide now, or has attempted suicide in the past, his potential for killing himself is greatly increased. The attempt at suicide may be a 'cry for help'. It is better to take the risk of suicide in a client seriously than play down its importance.

As a care worker, any anxiety you feel about a client's potential for suicide should be passed to a supervisor. The client may require some skilled specialist help from a psychiatrist, doctor or mental health worker. Some social workers are specially trained to assess the severity of the risk.

The effects of a death by suicide are much worse for relatives and friends than the effects of any other type of death. The survivors are left facing difficult questions for which there are no easy answers. They have to cope with a mixture of unresolved emotions towards the deceased person, among them a feeling of guilt because they could not prevent him taking his own life. If there were problems in the relationship with the person then the survivors are also left with any 'unfinished business' which they were unable to put right before the person died.

Sometimes people have negative feelings towards the survivors of a suicide and behave as if they drove the person to commit the act, either by lack of care or by failure to act on the signs of his distress. Family friends may wonder if the suicide's possible mental illness means other members of the family are likely to become mentally ill as well. Family survivors may feel stigmatised by these ideas but at the same time worry that they might be true and that some day they themselves might be driven to suicide.

As a result of the stress they are under survivors may deny that the death was suicide. They may spend a lot of time trying to persuade people it was not suicide because they feel ashamed. If the family deny the truth it is impossible for individual members to come to terms with what has happened.

A death by suicide is not only difficult because it is sudden but also because people have to deal with powerful ambivalent feelings towards the deceased. It is difficult for the survivors to tolerate their strong feelings of love and hate at the same time. The act of suicide seems to imply that the person was rejecting the survivors and that there was nothing they could have done to make him believe living was worthwhile. The act may have been deliberately planned by the deceased to express his anger towards the survivors; for example, by shooting or hanging himself in a place where his spouse is the person most likely to find him.

If a death appears to be a suicide it has to be investigated so all the relatives are questioned closely. They may complain of harsh treatment because they feel they are being interrogated. Insurance companies may also question them to see if they are entitled to death benefits under the policy they hold.

Survivors who hold strong religious convictions may feel that by committing suicide the deceased person will be unable to go to heaven and will be separated from God. This means that they have no hope of being reunited with him and putting every thing right in their relationship.

The way the survivors, the police, the community and, sometimes, the church respond reminds bereaved people that the death was unnatural. This is very difficult for them to handle emotionally. For this reason, survivors greatly value the support of care workers who do not avoid the awkward aspect of death and who are willing to listen to their worries about it. Some survivors may find the strain of coping with the after-effects so great that they require referral for professional help, if this is allowed.

See Exercise 9.

EXERCISE 9

Try to work out what your own feelings about suicide are. Make brief notes on the occasions when you think suicide:

● could be justified

● could not be justified

SUDDEN DEATH

A sudden death is one which occurs without warning. An unexpected death is known to produce difficulties in the grieving process. It is also more difficult for care workers to cope with than a death which is expected. Many care workers worry about their own response to a sudden death and about how they will cope with the responses of relatives and friends.

People react to sudden death by expressing very strong emotions. They feel guilty and say things like:

'How could I have prevented this?'

'I should have been here. Then this wouldn't have happened. '

21

They also feel angry and may direct their anger towards the care workers by saying:

> 'How could you let this happen?'

> 'He was all right until he came here'

At the time of impact, that is, when the death occurs, denial is common. Some people protest and say that there has been a mistake:

> 'You've got the wrong person – my Billy can't be dead'.

> 'How can she be dead? I was only talking to her yesterday.'

It is difficult for everyone involved to accept the reality of the situation.

People also get upset about 'unfinished business' and have regrets about things they wished they could have said or done. They feel that if only they had known the person was going to die they would have been more caring or expressed their feelings of love.

As a care worker, knowing in theory what to expect is important, but you may also have to be present and to witness, or share, these feelings. This is not easy. In such situations, your role may be to assist or be present while relatives and friends are being cared for.

You must not expect to have answers that will make people feel better immediately. It is not possible for you to put things right for them and you should not tell them that things will be all right soon, or in a year's time. They may ask for this reassurance later, but at first what they need is to feel you are sharing the present moment with all its pain. Although you will find it difficult, your presence and your ability to stay with the pain of the present moment provide tremendous strength to people who are feeling shocked and upset. Later, when they are beginning to come to terms with the death, people are able to acknowledge how much they valued the support of the care worker who was able simply to stay with them and tolerate the intense distress they were feeling.

BREAKING BAD NEWS

Care workers may be present when relatives are given the news of someone's death. There are no special words to use that will make it easier to give such news. People are often surprised at the way in which relatives are told about a death. A short, clear message is usually given first, such as:

> 'I am very sorry, but I have bad news for you. Your wife has died'

> 'I am very sorry, the worst has happened – your daughter has died'

Most people value a short clear message about what has happened because they have sensed that something is terribly wrong. After the first clear statement has been made time should be allowed for questions to be asked. This may take a long time if the person is crying and in great distress, or if he is showing signs of withdrawal.

Some people sit stunned and are unable to speak for a while; they need someone to stay with them. Even if, as a care worker, you feel you are not doing anything it is important that they have your presence with them because this is a comfort in itself. Many people feel very frightened and isolated at that moment and your presence is needed to help them feel safe.

The words used to give the news of the death should be clear and not open to misinterpretation. 'Died' or 'dead' cannot be misinterpreted, as other words can.

Exercise 10 considers some of the other words we use for death.

EXERCISE 10

Make a list of words that can be used to indicate that a person has died.

For example, *'Passed over'*, *'Kicked the bucket'* or *'Gone to meet his maker'*, You may be surprised at how many there are. You will probably strongly dislike some of them!

CHILDREN, ADOLESCENTS AND GRIEF

In Western families children are often excluded from the events surrounding a death. Adults want to protect them from some of the nasty things in life. This may be because they want to keep them innocent and unspoiled; they may feel that contact with death would 'contaminate' them with the stark reality of life, in the same way as sex 'contaminates' them and removes their innocence. But the desire to prevent children experiencing the effects of death delays their growing understanding of life.

Young children are often sent away to relatives when there is a death in the family. This means they do not have to be involved in the rituals of death, such as funerals. Adults may try to hide talk of death from children – as well as any crying or distress – if they think these things will be harmful to them.

When a person dies children sometimes fear that he has just disappeared because the adults have failed to involve them in the death or allow them to be part of the rituals surrounding it. Fortunately, there is now a shift away from this protective response which adults use not only to protect children but also to avoid being asked awkward questions themselves. Some of the questions children ask about death are very difficult to answer and they force adults to face issues they would rather push to one side. For example:

'Why did Daddy die and leave us behind? Was he cross with us?'

'When he is cremated how long will it take to make him into ashes?'

'Why can't we go and find Mummy again and bring her back?'

Children need to know as many details about the death as they are mentally equipped to process; the amount of information needed will depend on the individual child. Children ask questions if they are interested and feel that adults are willing to listen to whatever they say with an open mind.

Children need to grieve as well as have answers to their questions; again, the process varies according to their age. Although children are naturally inquisitive they can only process small pieces of information. They need to return to the subject frequently in their attempt to understand what it means. Some young children ask questions daily for months about the death of a brother, sister or other member of the family. The great need children have to talk and ask questions about the deceased is a very important way for them to try to understand what has happened. It is also important that the adult's response is warm and caring, and that he is receptive to everything the child asks. Adults must not answer the child in a way that suggests he has been bad. The child may have wished someone (especially a brother or sister) would go away or die, but he must be reassured that his wishes were not granted by the death. This feeling is often described as 'survivor guilt' and is not only felt by siblings (brothers and sisters) but also by the parents of children who die. The parents may feel the child died because they did not protect him enough.

Children usually set the level of questions and ask only what they need to know. Many children are left to themselves rather than encouraged to reveal their grief. Children need to grieve but they also need help to discover their own responses to grief – they should not have adult responses imposed on them.

In families where people are used to sharing their feelings with one another it is easier to accept the open expression of emotions when a death occurs. In families where feelings have to be hidden or controlled people find it more difficult to move usefully through the process of grieving. Children are allowed to have negative feelings in an open family so they can express anger that the person has left or abandoned them. They are free to respond to the death with anger because the person who has gone has made everyone unhappy.

The open expression of feelings allows adults and children to become closer and more intimate with one another. Sometimes children express their grief through aggressive behaviour as well as by sadness. It helps children if an adult can sensitively explore their deepest fears and imaginings, which are usually far worse than the reality of the situation.

It can be especially difficult for adolescents to deal with grief. They would like to be treated as adults, but they also long to be comforted and cared for as they were when they were children. They may feel uncomfortable exposing their feelings to their friends or be unable to finds words to express their grief. Some adolescents have new roles and responsibilities thrust upon them when a family member dies; others may feel obliged to take on a new role.

See Exercise 11

EXERCISE 11

How would a 14-year-old boy – the eldest son in his family – be affected if his father dies? The changes in his life, and the roles he has to assume, will depend on things like his family's circumstances and the number of brothers and sisters he has.

However, in general terms, try to make some notes about the ways in which his life will alter and the difficulties he might face.

Some adolescents feel angry because their parents try to protect them from talk about a death or try to prevent them from seeing the body. They feel they are adult enough not to be treated this way and that their self-esteem is being undermined.

Grief in childhood and adolescence can be a very lonely experience, either because the young person is excluded or because parents, or others, are so occupied with their own grief that the child or adolescent is ignored. In later life, grief which has not been expressed in adolescence or childhood may emerge in various forms, such as illness or depression. Death affects the whole family and the needs of each family member should be recognised.

EMERGING FROM GRIEF

People begin to emerge from grief at different times depending on the circumstances of the death. Some people are left feeling damaged and are never able to live as full a life as they did before; other people find ways of making the loss manageable in a year or two, although this process can take several years.

The way a person sees himself has to change after a death and also the way he sees himself in relation to others; his role in life may be altered, particularly in the family. The outcome is also affected by the person's past experiences of pain, separation and other life crises, and how these were handled.

People's emergence from grief can be measured in different ways; for example, by the return of appetite, or of physical and social activities, and by the reawakening of sexual and other interests. Some of this renewed interest in life produces feelings of guilt but these are resolved eventually.

At first, the grief seems to invade every part of life from waking to sleeping, but in time the bereaved person begins to gain control over his grief responses. When this happens people often feel they are 'beginning to live again'. In fact, they have gone through the grieving process and are beginning to live with their loss. The loss becomes part of their life experience and they enter a new phase of life – life will not be the same again. People stop longing for what they had previously and begin life from a new standpoint; life can be exciting and stimulating again but in a different way from before.

SUMMARY EXERCISE

In his article 'Positive approaches to dying', John Branter encourages people to develop a more positive approach to death. He says that all relationships begin with strangers, and all end in death, separation, grieving and suffering, but it is these relationships alone which give life its meaning.

What do you think about this view of relationships? Do you agree that having a satisfying relationship with someone makes it worth taking the risk of being vulnerable to the effects of loss?

---

3 Dying

Dying is not the same as death. Death is the *end* of human life; dying is the *process* of life coming to an end. It is important to remember that dying is still a part of living; what makes it unique is the fact that it results in death.

This chapter looks at working with, and caring for, those who are dying and those – including care workers – who are close to them. How much should the dying client, and his family and friends, be told about what is happening to him? Who cares for the care worker, in her pain and distress? We also consider the final part of the dying process and discuss some of the fears associated with it.

We explored some of the fears, anxieties and uncertainties connected with dying when we looked at the effect on individuals of retirement, moving house and changing jobs (see pages 4 and 6). You may find it difficult to compare dying with any of these life changes. However, like these events, dying interferes with our ability to function in familiar ways. We become comfortable – and perhaps feel safe – with certain well-established patterns of living. We find it disturbing when we are asked to do something different and leave the wellworn, repetitive patterns of life we are used to.

Think about some of the things you do regularly every day, like your journey to work – travelling on the same bus, turning the same corners and looking at the same view. One day, because of road works, the bus takes a different route. The change of route may be necessary, but you may still find it worrying and ask yourself questions like:

> *'Will I be late for work?'*

> *'What happens if the driver gets lost because he is away from his familiar route?'*

> *'What will happen to those people who normally catch the bus further on?'*

The change of route may make you very anxious, but if there are no problems and the bus arrives on time you may decide that it makes a nice change to travel on a different route!

See Exercise 11.

EXERCISE 11

Think about a day when your familiar routine was altered by a change in events.

It could be because of something very simple, like forgetting your house key and being locked out of the house, or responding to a fire alarm at work with all the upset that involves.

Write a short account about what happened, describing how you felt and how you responded to the change.

When you have finished Exercise 11 you may have a better understanding of the extremes of feeling involved in a change of routine. It can be irritating, frightening or exciting. Imagine the guilt and distress people go through when they feel these emotions during their involvement with someone who is

27

dying. They may not have any previous experience of dealing with the death of a close relative or friend. Many different questions worry them:

'Can dead people think?'

'Will he be able to see me when he has gone?'

'Is there another life?'

'Where will she go?'

'What will it be like after death?'

These questions are not easy to understand or answer. People who spend time with the dying person may need long periods of reflection to think about the issues raised by dying and death. It may be the first time that some people have ever given these questions any attention.

Although the death of each individual is a unique event, death itself is a universal experience because it happens to every living person. Each society and culture develops its own beliefs and rituals for coping with death.

THE FACT OF DEATH

Most people give some thought to the fact that they will die. When people are healthy, or not involved with anyone else's death, they have various ways of dealing with dying. One way is to make dying a universal event which no one can avoid:

'Everybody has to die'

'Every 2 or 3 minutes someone dies somewhere in the world'

'We all begin to die from the moment we are born'

'We all have to go sometime'

This is an abstract way of speaking about death which people use when they are not closely involved with it – they do not feel the same once they are personally involved.

Do you think this is true? Try Exercise 12.

EXERCISE 12

Look again at the above statements and add another sentence to each one which shows you do not want to be involved with dying or death. For example:

'Everybody has to die . . . but I do not want it to be anybody who belongs to me.'

'Every 2 or 3 minutes someone dies somewhere in the world . . .

'We all begin to die from the moment we are born . . .

**'We all have to go sometime . . .

Our views about dying vary depending on whether we are thinking about our own or someone else's dying. When you think about your own dying you can ask yourself searching questions which you would not ask other people, for example:

'When will I begin to die?'

'Will I be young or old?'

'How long will it take?'

'Will it be a long, painful experience?'

'Will I be alone?

Will I be in control?'

It is essential that people know how much control they will have over what happens to them when they are dying. The psychological pain involved in dying is difficult to deal with, but fear of physical pain can cause people just as much anxiety.

THE PROBLEM OF PAIN

Most people are frightened of dying in pain themselves arid do not want to watch a loved one suffer a painful death. Severe pain makes people feel helpless and distressed; it reminds them that they are not in control of the situation, particularly if they depend on others for relief. If possible, it is better if a client can control his own pain relief. However, some of the drugs used to control pain are subject to strict security measures and this may be one reason why a client or patient cannot have total control over his own pain relief, especially in institutional settings like hospitals.

A client's fears about pain can be reduced by promises that, at all times, his pain will be controlled. It is important that these promises are kept. Specialist nurses, such as Macmillan nurses, know a great deal about pain control and care of the dying. They can reassure clients and suggest different ways of coping with pain.

Each individual responds differently to pain and we should not make judgements about clients' reactions. What one person thinks of as a trivial injury may make someone else rush to the medicine cupboard for a painkiller. The important thing about pain control is that the client feels secure that his need for pain-controlling drugs will be met.

Care workers may feel anxious in case they have to help decide whether a client needs further drugs or if he should have them. Most health care professionals now let the client choose, perhaps by helping him decide how severe the pain is.

Figure 2
Pain scale

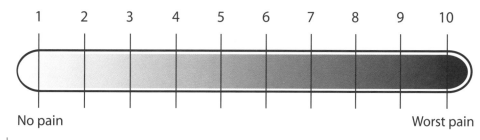

29

For example, a client may be asked to use a scale like the one shown in Figure 2. The client is asked to point to where his pain comes on the scale. This can be charted, to check whether one part of the day is worse than another and to evaluate the usefulness of the drugs being used. The treatment given depends on the individual's assessment of his needs, that is, his judgement or opinion. There are other ways of evaluating a client's pain. The position of his body can show restlessness, tension, discomfort and a reluctance to move. Sometimes a client's facial expression is an obvious clue to the pain they are feeling.

See Exercise 13A.

EXERCISE 13A

Try to remember a time when you were in pain.

Do not write down what caused the pain, but describe how it felt in note form or with a list.

What bodily positions did you adopt? (for example, curled up)

What behaviour was an indication of your pain? (for example, crying) .

After making your list or brief notes, write 'I was in pain with . . .' and describe your painful condition.

Look again at the feelings, bodily signs and behaviour you have described.

If you had seen these signs in another person would you have known that he was in pain and what was causing it?

It is not always easy to make useful assessment of another person's pain, and a client may become angry if we fail to respond to him. A client also needs to know that his own threshold of pain will be accepted and that care workers will not think he is exaggerating his pain or think of him as cowardly or weak. He is the one experiencing the pain so he should know!

Fear of pain returning causes tension in a client's body, which increases the pain and makes it more difficult to control. It also produces distress and frustration because the return of the pain is out of the client's control. There are many useful drugs available which can be prescribed on a regular basis to prevent pain recurring.

Other methods of controlling pain apart from the use of drugs are now considered acceptable. At one time these methods were called 'alternative medicine,' but now they are available as part of the client's complete care. Some people say they only offer a diversion which takes the client's mind off the pain for a while. But if he finds these methods helpful, why not use them? They include:

- aromatherapy
- reflexology
- relaxation exercises
- use of music
- acupuncture
- massage.

See Exercise 13B.

EXERCISE 13B

Find out about one of the methods of alternative or complementary medicine listed and write a short account of how it may help a client control his pain.

PSYCHOLOGICAL SUPPORT

The process of dying brings many losses for the client and his family – loss of job, loss of goals, loss of role and, eventually, loss of life itself. The emotional response to these losses is known as grief. Before a loss takes place people may experience anticipatory grief. If a family's anticipatory grief leads them to resolve their grief before the client's death he will feel abandoned. The family members may then feel guilty and frustrated.

Certain stages of grief are particularly associated with anticipatory grief. Elizabeth Kübler-Ross has outlined five stages of grieving which, in anticipating his loss; the client and his relatives may work through:

- denial and isolation
- anger
- bargaining
- depression
- acceptance

"anticipatory grief" the range of feelings experienced by client, family and significant others when they expect (anticipate) a loss

31

DENIAL AND ISOLATION

A state of numbness and withdrawal may follow the diagnosis of a terminal illness (that is, the last stage of a fatal disease). All clients use different degrees of denial, not only when the illness is first diagnosed, but also in its later stages. The denial and need for isolation give the client space in which to gather together some resources for handling the situation.

As care workers we may be anxious about the client's need to be alone, but we must respect both his need to reflect on the seriousness of his position and his efforts to find ways of managing the situation. If the client can start to do this it will help him regain control of events.

However, we also need to recognise when withdrawal and isolation becomes self-defeating.

This is when we see that the client is alone, scared or angry. The care worker can be very useful to the client during this first stage, when he begins to talk about what is happening. Talking helps the client to work out his feelings about dying and deal with his denial.

ANGER

Anger often follows denial and isolation. The client becomes angry because he feels helpless and frustrated at not being in control of his life or destiny. He may direct the anger towards himself for not looking after himself or towards the care workers. He may complain about lack of care or resources, or about his family and the world in general.

It is upsetting to see someone become increasingly bitter and irritable about what has happened to him. Family, friends and loved ones may complain to the care worker that they never seem to get anything right and that the client is saying hurtful things to them. As a care worker you may have to explain how anger is often an expression of someone's pain or distress, and that it is not always easy to identify the source of the hurt.

BARGAINING

During this stage the client tries to find something that will postpone his death or put things right. He may believe that if he gives up previous wrongdoings he will make amends and prevent his death. Some clients use the care worker as a kind of priest and confess their past wrongdoings to her. This is a useful way of ending unfinished business for some clients but for others it is a way of bargaining for their life. Some couples promise never to argue or fight again in an attempt to prevent a child from dying. Bargaining can be shown when people say things like:

> *'If only I could turn the clock back'*

> *'Tell me what to do to put this right'*

> *'I feel responsible and want to put this right'*

Some people feel that if they behave well they will extend life and remove pain. Sometimes when a person is dying old family quarrels are pushed aside and people are reconciled. Most people make their bargains secretly with God; Kübler-Ross describes this as 'doing a deal with God.'

DEPRESSION

When the client is no longer able to deny the existence of his illness he feels a great sense of loss. The point at which he can no longer deny the illness may be when a marked weight loss or some other deteriorating condition becomes obvious and he needs to have more intensive treatment than before. The client sees his job and family roles change, and realises the hopelessness of his dreams and future plans. He prepares himself for the separation and loss to come. There is anticipatory grief at this stage because the painful reality cannot be avoided. The client is beginning to prepare himself for death and will often seem to be surrounded by sadness.

ACCEPTANCE

If the client has been given enough time and support to work through the first four stages he may reach the stage where he accepts that he is going to die. He puts aside past struggles and conflicts and is more at peace with himself. This acceptance is a relief for the client and everyone concerned with his welfare. The care worker can now take on a quieter more passive role with the client, as he is no longer struggling to put things right in his life in the same way. She may be able to spend longer periods in silence and unspoken caring – sitting with a dying client, holding his hand or just being with him. Most care workers have to learn to be comfortable with this less busy, more passive role. At this stage care workers often feel that the difficulties and trials of working through the other stages have been worthwhile.

Not all clients go through all these stages or they may not go through them in the order described. A client may pass back and forth through the stages or accept death without experiencing any of them. Some people never accept death and right to the end they live in hope that all will be put right. Although everyone has their own way of coping with death the five stages described by Kübler -Ross are common to many people. If you can recognise the stage a person is at you will be able to make and maintain contact with him.

WORKING WITH A DYING PERSON

Both the type of illness and the process of dying limit the time you have in which to establish a good understanding with the client. You may feel under pressure to come up with quick answers or to get things sorted out rapidly. But denial, anger and the other responses described above cannot be sorted out quickly and easily. Care workers must be careful not to force the client to work through his difficulties. He may not even want them to be resolved.

Some short-term illnesses give a client only a few weeks or months to prepare for death and you may have to assist him in coping with this. A long-term fatal illness may mean you have months or even years to help your client prepare for death.

The dying client should decide the pace at which things are dealt with. He should not be forced to confront the issues he faces. Very few people sort out all life's difficulties before they die. People build protective walls around themselves and it does not help them if you try to break these down by being aggressive and using confrontation. No one wants to be left feeling exposed and vulnerable – it is easier for people to accept change if the walls of their defences against it are taken down brick by brick.

The way in which people die has changed over the past decade. The use of modern treatment and technology has brought about a reduction in fatal acute infections but an increase in more chronic conditions. For example, an acute infection such as pneumonia is less likely to be fatal nowadays; but although it can be treated it may recur repeatedly as a chest infection and eventually become a chronic condition. People may die slowly over many years because of a chronic condition like this.

Chronic illness can also result in people losing the use of various parts of their bodies over the years. The loss of ability they suffer can also lead to the loss of friends and business associates whose activities they can no longer share. This can be very frustrating for people; they are alive yet not able to live as full a life as they used to. Some clients become socially isolated because of chronic illness and this may result in a lonely death.

See Exercise 14.

EXERCISE 14

Write a few notes describing how someone with chronic chest disease could become socially isolated.

THE FAMILY

Some families insist that no one should discuss dying with the client. They put a great deal of energy into pretending that everything will be all right and everyone works hard at avoiding the real issues (see Figure 3).

Most dying people eventually learn the truth about their situation. However, they should be free to learn the details of their illness or condition. People acknowledge the facts about dying at a pace at which they can handle them. They may hear what others are saying and observe what is happening but filter out any information they are not ready to accept. People can subconsciously know the truth over a long period before admitting it to themselves and being open about it with others.

The person who recognises the fact of his death, but who is not allowed to share it for fear of hurting relatives, will feel isolated and lonely. No one should have to suffer in this way at a time when he may need the comfort and closeness of a loved one. Neither can care workers agree to relatives' wishes that they do not discuss dying or death if the client opens up the subject with them. They need to make it clear that they will have to respond sensitively to these issues with their clients because they cannot leave them alone with such difficulties. Lots of energy can be wasted guarding secrets or supporting the first lie. People feel hurt and angry when the truth emerges. It may be that a client would have chosen to live differently if he had known all the facts earlier, but no one can give him back the time that has been lost.

I huddle warm inside my corner bed
Watching the other patients sipping tea.
I wonder why I'm so long getting well,
And why it is no one will talk to me.

The nurses are so kind. They brush my hair
On days I feel too ill to read or sew.
I smile and chat, try not to show my fear,
They cannot tell me what I want to know.

The visitors come in. I see their eyes
Become embarrassed as they pass my bed.
'What lovely flowers,' they say, then hurry on
In case their faces show what can't be said.

The chaplain passes on his weekly round
With friendly smile and calm, untroubled brow.
He speaks with deep sincerity of Life;
I'd like to speak of Death, but don't know how.

The surgeon comes, with student retinue,
Mutters to sister, deaf to my silent plea.
I want to tell this dread I feel inside,
But they are all too kind to talk to me.

ANONYMOUS

Figure 3
Tell me the truth

Some clients do not wish to see or hear what is happening. They choose not to know, despite being given information, and this can be seen as an informed choice. To push people into what they do not want to see or hear, or what they want to deny, is as cruel and inhumane as a conspiracy of silence.

Some families find that the experience of a person dying brings them closer together; for others, it increases family conflict. In general, close, caring families remain that way when a member is dying and families with poor relationships have them stretched to the limit. Family members often feel regret that it was only when one of them was near to death that they were able to value each other.

Try Exercise 15

EXERCISE 15

Make notes for each of the following.

When a family member is dying:

● what might people realise they regret?

● what past family difficulties may emerge?

Occasionally, a client uses dying as a way of controlling members of his family. He will appear to be dying at important times in the life of the family, such as times of impending change. The client, by saying or implying that he is dying, is able to exert some control over what family members do. You can read more about helping families in Skills for Caring – Families and Groups.

DYING AT HOME

Many families are now able to care for a dying person at home, a change encouraged by the influence of the hospice movement which provides specially trained staff to care for and support people at home. A client may feel more contented dying at home because it offers privacy and relatives are more comfortable with the familiar surroundings.

Home care is only possible with proper planning and consultation with all involved. It must also include the client's wishes. The family may need to be taught some new skills, such as how to make an occupied bed or how to feed someone who is helpless. Care workers must not assume family members can do these things.

If families are asked to take on more than they can manage they feel trapped and become resentful. Care workers may become involved because a family caring for a dying person at home need to have the chance of a break or time to go shopping.

Giving this kind of support to families lets them know that people recognise the stress they are under. They need to be given encouragement and credit for what they are doing. Care workers can do this by telling them what a great job they are doing under such difficult circumstances.

On many occasions families need someone to sit with a person who is very ill. This is an invaluable break for the relatives, giving them time to talk to others about the distress they are feeling.

Setting up home care, with the appropriate people needed to make it manageable, requires careful thought and planning. Some of the questions that should be explored first are shown in the panel: you may be able to add some more yourself.

Nurses who have special expertise in the care of the dying at home will provide care for all who need support, not just the client. The local authority may fund Macmillan or Marie Curie nurses, by health care services or by charitable funding. The care provided could include hospice care as an in-patient, or day care at the hospice.

Hospices also provide specially trained staff to care for people at home. This care extends beyond physical care and pain relief to providing psychological care and support. Many hospices extend their care to the period after the patient has died, to help the bereaved with grief. Some families may decide they want to help others in a similar situation and become involved in fund raising as a way of expressing thanks as well as working through their grief.

See Exercises 16 and 17.

CARE OF THE DYING AT HOME

- Who will care for the client?
- Who will care for the carers?
- Which rooms will be suitable and accessible for care and equipment?
- Would a hospital bed be useful?
- How will they manage large amounts of laundry and is help available for this?
- Are people in the home prepared for this drastic change to their lifestyle?
- Did the family make the decision?
- Does this care extend to the family after the client has died?

EXERCISE 16

Find out what statutory and charitable organisations are available in your area. What kind of support and help do they offer to the client dying at home and to his family?

EXERCISE 17

Think about your own home, who lives in it and the activity that goes on there?

Imagine what it would be like if one room was taken over by a hospital bed, a commode, incontinence pads and all the other equipment needed to care for a person dying at home.

Can you imagine what would it be like if you had to care for someone who is dying?

Make two lists, side by side, of the **advantages** and **disadvantages** of caring for someone who is dying at home.

CHARACTERISTICS OF THE CARE WORKER

Do care workers need any special qualities to care for a dying person? Some people believe that only those who have some experience of the death of others will be able to work usefully with the dying. Care staff often feel they have to apologise because no one they know has died, as if this would give them some qualification for dealing with dying. Remember, however, that a care worker's own encounter with dying may not have been a positive one. There is no doubt that this experience may increase her personal empathy with the client, but all care workers can learn to work with dying effectively if they want to.

"empathy"
the ability to share imaginatively the feelings of another person and communicate this understanding to him or her

To work with the dying, care workers need a knowledge of the dying process and its various stages. They must try to meet the needs of the dying and those close to them, and this requires some knowledge of expected patterns of behaviour connected with grief.

It is important that care workers use their skills to develop open, honest relationships with the client and his family. They will share some very intimate moments with them and need to know when to withdraw.

Every care worker has to examine her own feelings and attitudes towards death and dying because these attitudes will be reflected in her care. How she values life, death and health, her faith, and her thoughts on the meaning of life will be challenged. It is essential that a care worker accepts the client's response to these subjects even though it may be different from her own.

As a care worker, you might think, 'Yes, I will be able to accept my client's response', but in practice you will find that it is not an easy thing to do. Your own feelings of conflict or fear may make you avoid these issues with the client. Failure to work out your own beliefs and values may result in your emotional and physical care of the client being inadequate.

Care workers caring for the dying and their families need extra training. In a situation where there is a continuous outpouring of difficult feelings and needs, the care worker needs help for herself. Further reading and attending workshops will give her time away from the situation to explore the continuing stresses of the work.

Clients, families and other loved ones confide in their care workers. This can make care workers feel good or they can feel it is a burden. Talking about dying is not easy; the client can feel fearful and awkward. He may want to protect his family from his difficult and painful need to talk about the situation and choose his care worker instead. He will not necessarily be searching for pity or sympathy but simply for someone who has the ability to stay with his pain and difficulty and not shrug it off.

The client may be uncomfortable with the helplessness of his loved ones; he may feel the need to protect them from the final confirmation that he is dying. People often fear that if you talk about death it will happen so they avoid discussing it. Their inability to face death and dying may come from this kind of superstition or from long held, unspoken family traditions.

⁕confidante⁕
a female confidant, that is, a person who is entrusted with secrets

The care worker's role as confidante will involve listening and reassuring as the client grapples with his experience of dying. He may need help to decide what must be done and said before he dies, particularly regarding family relationships.

A dying person may be selective, and choose one member of the care team to confide in rather than another. Care workers must be prepared for this response and continue to provide opportunities for the client to share with them if he wishes. A care worker who gives the client the opportunity to select her as a confidante cannot – and should not demand that he does choose her.

All these aspects of a care worker's role can be enriching but they can also be distressing. On a personal level you, as a care worker, may experience feelings of grief and loss. You may need help with this, particularly support from your loved ones. For various reasons, they may not be able to offer this and other avenues of care and support will need to be explored. Some care workers set up their own support systems, with the help of others.

SUPPORT SYSTEMS FOR CARE WORKERS

Employers, supervisors and colleagues should make it clear to care workers where they can obtain support in caring for the dying. This is not entirely the responsibility of the management and the system, however; everyone has a responsibility to care for themselves and their colleagues. No one should be ashamed to ask for help. Involvement in the care of the dying is not easy and it makes many demands upon care workers. If they acknowledge the stress of the work it does not mean they are weak, inadequate or incapable stress is a normal response to the pressures involved.

PAIRING

Pairing is one way for colleagues to offer support to one another. Each worker is paired with another who is willing to offer a listening ear and, perhaps, a home phone number. Each seeks out the other on a regular basis – for example, by having lunch together – to check whether the work they are doing is manageable.

GROUP MEETINGS

Regular group meetings are another way to share difficulties. These can focus on coping with the emotional and practical difficulties of the work and can include occasions when speakers are invited to talk about related topics. Some care workers are more comfortable with a mixture of events because it means they are not concentrating entirely on the stresses of their work. From time to time, group members may also want to relax together by arranging social outings, perhaps to the theatre or for a meal.

It should always be emphasised that the purpose of these meetings is to care for the workers and that they have been set up because the organisation values them and their contribution. The meetings are not meant to improve efficiency or productivity, although this may be something which happens anyway as a result of the group meeting regularly.

When a new group forms it should lay down some ground rules, that is, rules of procedure for the group to follow, Some groups exclude managers or invite an outside, impartial facilitator to ensure the smooth running of the group. The ground rules shown in the panel on page 42 may be useful if you become involved in starting a group.

Colleagues should 'keep an eye' on a difficult family, or a death that confronts a care worker with some personal fear. It is essential that care workers care for each other in such a situation. Adequate rest and relaxation is important and they should seek this for themselves and their co-workers. Care workers may want to be available to the client and his family 24 hours a day, but this would be harmful to the care worker as a person.

Care workers should look after themselves and each other, and let someone know when they feel stressed. It is often difficult for people to see this for themselves, but no one should be ashamed to ask for help. Any help needed should be readily available or organised as required.

THE FINAL ACT OF DYING

What they learn from the media may colour people's images of death. Films and plays often show dying people screaming and shouting, rolling about cursing someone or begging for forgiveness. Sometimes people who are about to die are shown putting everything right just before death, or revealing all their fears and feelings. Certainly, many deathbed scenes show people gaining powerful insights just before their death.

The reality is that most people gently and quietly lose consciousness, go to sleep and die. Modem care, nursing skills and pain control usually ensure that this happens.

There are many views on what is a 'good' or 'bad' death. You may think, 'How can a death be good?' Perhaps dying with dignity, without pain and in the company of loved ones, is the ideal 'good' death – the part of living which comes at the end of a continuum. A death may be seen as good if people were getting on well with one another before the death occurred and if everything possible was done for the person right up to the last minute of his life.

The timing of a person's death also influences how people feel about it:

> 'He had no more fight left in him '
>
> 'She had given up the struggle'
>
> 'He had achieved so much in life '
>
> 'All her children were settled and happy so she was ready to go'

The dying and the death should bring a sense of a life being fulfilled and completed. The nature of the, death, and the circumstances following the death, affect the grieving process – the final act cannot be seen in isolation from the whole process.

Although many people fear facing the actual death and being confronted with the dead person, there is more to fear in the earlier stages of dying. As they emerge from grief, most people find, in looking back, that some of the worst pain was in the grief of knowing the person was dying rather than in being present at the moment of death itself.

REVIEW

Individuals respond to death in different ways. Dying is the final stage of life and it is important to associate this stage with health. In other words, the way individuals react to dying and death affects their physical and emotional wellbeing. The care worker who uses her knowledge of the dying process contributes to this wellbeing. Her skills can help people share difficult feelings and can ease the move towards grief. The process of grieving is necessary if the person is to emerge from the pain of death. Care workers are most useful to the client and his family if they are realistic. They cannot stop the process of dying or bring the person back; they cannot take away the pain of the loss. But they can reach out to the person's pain and grief if they accept that these responses are a natural part of the process.

SUMMARY EXERCISE

Summarise your own thoughts on what might make a good death.

GROUND RULES FOR GROUP SESSIONS

- Everyone who is here belongs here just because he is here and for no other reason.

- For each person, what is true is determined by what is in him, what he directly feels and finds making sense in himself; and the way he lives Inside himself.

- Our first purpose is to make contact with each other. Everything else we want or need comes second.

- We try to be as honest as possible, and to express ourselves as we really are and feel – just as much as we can.

- We listen for the person inside. living and feeling.

- We listen to everyone.

- The group leader is responsible for two things only: he protects the belonging of every member, and he protects their being heard if this is getting lost.

- Realism – if we know things are a certain way, we do not pretend they are not that way.

- What we say here is confidential. No one will repeat anything said her' outside the group, unless it concerns only himself. This applies not just to obviously private things, but to everything. If the individual concerned wants others to know something, he can always tell them himself.

- Decisions made by the group need everyone taking part in some way.

- New members become members because they walk in and remain. Whoever is here belongs

(Gendlin & Beebe 1968).

4 Bereavement and Loss

This chapter explores some of the issues involved in bereavement and loss in more detail. The last part of the chapter looks at funerals and the rituals surrounding death, and considers their use to individuals and society.

Working with loss is a major part of any care worker's day. Many of the losses she deals with have lasting effects on people's lives. For example, a woman feels deeply the loss involved in a mastectomy and hysterectomy because the parts of her body affected are connected with sexuality, reproduction and her understanding of herself as a woman. Losses can occur because of changes to the body. Some changes are obvious, for example, the removal of a limb. Other changes may not be as obvious but are equally important, such as the removal of internal organs or a sensory loss. A change in the organs associated with excretion can be distasteful for many people and difficult for them to tolerate. People's response to alterations to their image can threaten their status and role in life.

BODY IMAGE

Our body image is our view of ourselves. As we grow and walk about this view of ourselves becomes well established, and is fixed by the end of adolescence. Young people receive messages that give them an image of how others see their body. They may be described as:

- cute
- weak
- strong
- pretty
- plain
- awkward
- good
- bad
- ugly
- clumsy.

Many people think a person's body is the most important expression of who they are as an individual. At vulnerable times, like the years when we are growing into adulthood, we are strongly influenced by messages from our peer group (our equals) about our appearance. Our peers express values about one another according to looks, body, clothes and style. The media and advertisers who suggest ways to achieve and maintain our attractiveness by having a youthful, healthy appearance exploit these early messages.

See Exercise 18.

EXERCISE 18

Look at the advertisements shown during three of the commercial breaks on television.

Make a list of items being sold which are said to improve your body image and list the words used. Remember, this applies not only to clothes and cosmetics but also to cars and holidays.

The ideal body image and the way you see your own body image become associated with your idea of your physical appearance. It is the body others see that demonstrates your skills and abilities; these, in turn, reveal your emotions. This means that your awareness of your own body image has important emotional consequences.

Your body image is open to change. Its shape, size, how it is structured and how it functions may alter. This can happen slowly, and may not be obvious, or it can be sudden and dramatic. Your hair may gradually turn grey and lines appear on your face; you may be aware of this or choose to deny it. Some people make these changes part of their view of themselves; others deny them and then experience a sudden feeling of crisis or loss at the change. People often comment on a person's need to preserve parts of their body or retain its image:

'Did you know he wears a wig?'

'She is really very grey and dyes her hair.'

EXAMPLE

Evelyn was 50 years old and worked as a buyer of fashionable clothes for a large department store. She had to make predictions about future trends in fashion and take risks when calculating the volume of certain clothes she bought. Evelyn had always felt that her personal appearance (her body image) was very Important to her overall performance and ability. She became preoccupied with the lines in the skin on her face and when some of her fashion predictions were wrongly timed she began to worry that she was losing her ability and judgement. She told herself she was getting old and that she was no longer efficient.

Evelyn decided that she needed to have cosmetic surgery to alter her image. She was sure that after surgery she would return to her former self and once again experience the energy and skill she had known when she was younger. What Evelyn failed to see was that the real problem was not her wrinkles but the fact that she was out of touch with current trends. She had lost some of her former contacts, with whom she could discuss forthcoming changes in the market, and was miscalculating the moment when new styles and ideas emerged. Because Evelyn's expectations of the outcome of the surgery were wrong, when the change in her image failed to have the expected result in her life she blamed it on poor quality surgery. Soon she was involved in a longstanding dispute with the doctors, nurses and the health authority.

Some clients undergo cosmetic surgery with high hopes that the results will change their lives. However, it is not always possible for the results of surgery to meet people's expectations, as the example about Evelyn shows. How people think of the effects of an illness depends on how they cope with change. Changes in physical appearance, or in people's body image, result in changes in other areas of their lives too. Change involves leaving behind things that are familiar, accepted parts of our existence. Body image is closely associated with our feelings, inner beliefs and personal goals; our own ideas of our strengths and weaknesses are the result of the way we see our image. A change in a small area of a person's body, whether it is internal or external, can take on great significance, as it did for David in the following example.

EXAMPLE

David was brought into hospital, after being involved in a fight. He was a successful member of a public relations team, but had many personal problems. His wife had left him and he could not understand why, when he was such a success in business, he was a failure in his personal life. He could not see that his success in business was at the expense of his relationship with his wife.

David's drive and belief in his personal qualities gave him confidence. While spending the evening in a nightclub with his brother-in-law he became involved in a fight. David had a strong sense of what was right and wrong and asked two men who were making offensive remarks to a group of women to behave themselves. In the fight that followed he was thrown to the ground and his head was kicked. On arrival at the accident and emergency department he had a cut head and his two top front teeth were missing.

David was very distressed and crying openly. The staff checked that he was not in pain, but he kept saying *'They have knocked my teeth out. My God, how do I look?'* The wound on his head was sutured (stitched), but his distress about his teeth increased – to him the effects of this loss were enormous:

'How will I get my wife back now?'

'Who will want me?'

'I will be a failure at work'

No one will listen to me now'

No amount of reassurance could persuade him that two natural looking teeth could be made to replace the ones he had lost. His attitude caused the staff great difficulty and eventually he discharged himself from hospital.

David's confidence was built on his view of his body image. He believed that his success depended on how he looked. When his body image was (as he saw it) damaged, other painful feelings emerged; he felt that he deserved to suffer or that his injury was some kind of punishment.

Evelyn wanted a body change; David had a body change forced on him. Both examples show that the people concerned believed their strengths as individuals, and their goals in their private lives and at work, were centred around their image.

Some clients behave in a particular way after changes in bodily image. The feelings associated with these changes may be difficult for the care worker to cope with, as well as for the client's family and friends. For example, in the long-term the client may often choose to be by himself, taking time to reflect on things on his own. This desire for solitude is of great importance to the client, but it is a need which is often misunderstood by his family, friends and care workers. However, as long as they see that he has no immediate needs this time alone is useful for him. It usually follows the impact phase and the initial distress felt about the changes (see page 19). It would seem that the client re-evaluates himself in relation to the change and the time alone gives him the chance to come to terms with the change at his own pace.

It is not necessarily useful if lots of people are insisting the client is still the same and is still acceptable. He is not the same: he feels different and may look different. He has to make the change between who he was and who he is. In these situations it is very easy to try to reduce the size of the problem by saying things like:

> 'You are lucky if is not worse'
>
> 'What are you worrying about, you will soon get over it.'
>
> 'Looks are not everything'

Responses such as these are well meaning but take away from the painful feelings the client has as a result of the immediate impact of the change. He needs someone to validate his first reactions and fears, not reduce or dismiss them.

"validate"
to search for the meaning and emotion in a client's words and agree with him that this is how he feels

It would be easy to say that image is not important and that people value other aspects of a person much more. People say that other characteristics, such as loyalty, self-determination and creativity are more important, but in practice they often place more importance on image and appearance.

We have looked at how an injury can damage appearance and how the ageing process and the physical changes it brings can have serious emotional effects. It is sometimes suggested that physical appearance is less important to males than to females. However, we should not make assumptions about this, although some changes do have an obvious sexual connection.

MASTECTOMY

Removal of a breast can cause a woman a great deal of emotional distress as well as the feeling that she is now disfigured. As with any loss the woman needs to have an opportunity to grieve for her loss. The issue of her altered body should not be avoided either.

The decision to operate on a lump in the breast is usually made quickly. Decisions to perform other kinds of surgery are generally made to reduce pain caused by longstanding problems. It is helpful if both patient and doctor can take the time to discuss the decision and prepare for the operation. But if the decision to remove a breast has to be made quickly a woman can feel distressed at its urgency and may feel that she was not in control of what happened.

The issue of whether or not we control our lives, and have some say in what happens to us, often arises during a crisis situation. The speed at which a mastectomy occurs in a woman's life increases this sense of lost control. Pre-operative and post-operative counselling reduce some of the distress. It is also helpful if the woman's sexual partner can be included in the decision-making to increase her sense of retaining some power over the situation.

After the operation the woman may have unspoken anxieties about several issues and will need time to discuss these. The immediate issues, such as scarring or disfigurement, may be easy to talk about when the care worker is helping her to bathe or doing the dressings. But the client may find it difficult to talk openly of her fear of the cancer spreading further, or to ask whether the care worker has any information about this. It is very important that care workers allow the client to put these fears into words.

HYSTERECTOMY

Surgery for a hysterectomy, that is, surgical removal of the womb, also has great significance for a woman because of its association with her sexuality and body image. Many of the difficulties a woman has will be related to her age, marital status and social background but care workers should not make any assumptions. For example, if the client is beyond childbearing age we must not assume that the surgery will be less traumatic; when it takes place the client may also be dealing with one of the life milestones discussed on page ?.

Studies on hysterectomy again emphasise how pre-operative discussion, and satisfactory explanation of the issue involved, can lessen some of the psychological trauma attached to it. If the client seems puzzled, or is having difficulty in understanding all the effects of the operation, then you may have to provide her with more information. Increasing the client's knowledge about how her body works is a straightforward way of reducing her anxiety, so it is important that the care worker has some basic knowledge of how systems work. (Some helpful books on this subject are suggested in the reading list at the end of the book.)

ILEOSTOMY, COLOSTOMY AND ILEOCONDUIT

These procedures can be permanent or temporary and describe the making of an artificial anus from the colon, or urethra from the bladder, which then empties the body's waste products into a bag. This involves a definite change in outward appearance which is visible to the client and possibly to other people who are important to them.

The external changes are what clients find most distressing. Some of the surgery associated with the internal condition may also have distressing consequences later. It may be much easier to work with the change that can be seen first and, having helped the client accept it, begin to help them cope with the effects of the internal changes.

Extensive abdominal and perineal surgery can cause nerve damage in men, resulting in impotence. Surgery for ileoconduit may cause an orgasmic dysfunction called 'retarded ejaculation'. Problems such as this may need the special advice and the help of a psychosexual counsellor.

How people respond to the external changes is important. Attention will be directed at what most people regard as a private area and will also be focused on the process of excretion. Clients may have been taught as children that such matters were not to be discussed; having to discuss this may make the client feel like a child again. Clients need to have time to discuss questions about smell and the disposal of bags, or whether they can continue to function sexually. It is not possible to deal with all these issues quickly. The nature of the surgery and the post-operative period should give the client a chance to explore each issue separately, without overwhelming him with too many topics at once.

If the client shows a high level of anxiety about how the changes will damage a personal relationship it could be a sign that the relationship is already vulnerable. If this is the case, you may have difficulty concentrating on what is happening to the client at the time. If longstanding difficulties have come into the open because of the changes the client may need more intensive or prolonged marital therapy.

Again, the client needs to be able to talk about any worries he has about his prognosis, that is, the forecast of the course of his disease.

If the client is encouraged to touch the affected parts of his body and use his own strengths and inner resources, the negative side of the loss can be seen in proportion to its positive side. Also, if the client can involve someone who is important in his life it can help him overcome his early fears about coping with the change.

SENSORY ORGANS

The damage or loss of sensory organs, such as one or both eyes, may be sudden or part of a prolonged illness. In diabetes, for example, gradual loss of sight may be something that the client will either have come to terms with or compensate for in other ways. He may have known this was a possibility but suddenly realising the effect it will have on his life can cause great distress.

Sudden loss or damage of a sensory organ can be clearly seen by other people and gains their sympathy. But a loss like the gradual loss of hearing can result in social isolation. People become irritated and impatient because the client is unable to fully understand or respond to conversations. This can be very disheartening for the sufferer because he knows that people are thinking he is stupid. This reaction causes the client to withdraw from people and to put less and less effort into communicating with them.

The client may deliberately shut himself off from people because he feels unacceptable, imperfect or damaged. People who know him may say 'He is not the same person'. This may be true, but it could be that he is a different person because the people close to him are intolerant of his disability and unable to adapt to the loss which has caused the change in his character or lifestyle.

Skin

Damage to, or loss of, skin may have to be dealt with over a long period of time. People undergoing extensive or prolonged surgery become miserable about the time it takes and the continued pain and discomfort they have to go through. Others may have to accept that complete change is not possible but camouflage is.

To summarise, altered body image may:

- threaten a person's image or status
- change a familiar and long-accepted part of a person
- weaken a person's security by raising issues of whether he possesses, or has lost control of, what he assumed would always be his
- suddenly become difficult to cope with, after a long period of gradual change
- make people feel vulnerable and ill at ease with themselves and produce grief

RESPONDING TO ALTERED BODY IMAGE

It can be useful for a client to express concern and anxiety about body image. It is a way of exploring the possible effects of the change with another person. This outward expression of inner concerns is both necessary and healthy for many clients. The care worker can use the occasion to reassure the client that he is still acceptable and that she continues to recognise him as a person. Certain patterns of behaviour may follow bodily change, including:

- passivity
- denial
- reassurance
- isolation
- hostility.

PASSIVITY

If the client is passive he appears withdrawn and listless, simply accepting the care he is offered. His lowered morale and reduced self-esteem can lead to this sadness and withdrawal which may result in him not wanting to be involved in his own care. The client may feel that he is unacceptable and this can lead to him being poorly motivated and losing the will to take any part in deciding what happens to him.

DENIAL

The client may show denial by refusing to touch or look at an altered part of his body, such as a colostomy, operation scar or damaged tissue. If the client has had a limb amputated or a breast removed he or she may deny its absence. It can be very distressing for the care worker when the client resists her attempts to return his attention to the loss or change. The care worker then feels that by trying to do this she is inflicting pain and distress on the client, and worries that this may strain their relationship.

REASSURANCE

The client may seek constant attention from the care worker and from his family in order to reassure himself that he is still acceptable to them. He may make dismissive remarks like 'Nobody ever really fancied me anyway' to gain that reassurance. Giving the client a compliment can have a very powerful effect on these occasions because it lets him know that appearance or image does not take away from the attractiveness of the complete person.

ISOLATION

The client's isolation may be self-imposed because he feels unacceptable. He may feel that, rather than risk people's rejection, he will avoid them altogether. If the client says that he is less acceptable to family or friends, it is easy for the care worker to quickly deny it and say it is all in his imagination. However, the client may have sensed his family's response correctly. It is not unusual for family members or friends to reject a client because of bodily changes. They make remarks like:

'He is not the person that he was.'

'It has altered his personality.'

This could be true, but it could be that they themselves are unable to cope with the physical changes they see in the client. Their attitude to both the physical changes, and the changes in the client's emotional state, may be the reasons they are rejecting him.

HOSTILITY

Feelings of anger and hostility emerge continually when clients feel strongly about their altered or damaged body image. Their protest may be intended for someone else, but be directed at the care worker because she is there. If the client feels that some other person is responsible but cannot express his anger towards them, he may become rebellious or provocative towards the care worker.

Any of these changes in behaviour may occur after sudden death, as well as after the loss of a limb or organ, or a change in appearance. The loss of some organs also results in the loss of masculinity or femininity. These losses can result in as much grief as death does. **Try Exercise 19 now.**

EXERCISE 19

Write down some answers to the following questions (it may help to look at yourself in a full-length mirror before answering!).

How would you describe your appearance?

Describe in list form:

● what you like about your body

● what you dislike about your body.

What do you value most about your body and why?

If you could change anything about your body what would it be and how could it alter your life?

PHANTOM LIMB

Not all denial is in the mind of the client, that is, psychological. After an amputation the client may experience itching or pain in the limb, or feel that the limb is still attached to him. This is known as 'phantom limb' and it has a physiological explanation, that is, one to do with the body. Severed nerve endings continue to send messages to the brain and are interpreted as coming from the severed limb. Until the nerves heal fully, the client will continue to experience what seem to be irrational sensations. He knows the limb is missing, but his nervous system sends him messages that it is still present. If he is warned about this he will be reassured that he is not losing his sanity when he experiences it. Inflammation and irritation of an amputation site make this problem worse. Any measures to reduce itching and inflammation will reduce the effect of problems caused by phantom limb.

CANCER

Cancer may produce physical changes, such as disfigurement, pain, weakness and weight loss. People think of these things when they hear the word 'cancer' and connect them with a distorted body image. The statistics on cancer show that this is not always the case; skin cancer, for example, does not require major surgery and may not involve serious emotional changes.

It is important to remember that cancer does not always mean pain, disfigurement and death. Half the patients who have operations for lung cancer are cured. Relatives can be influenced by the distorted body image connected with cancer. For example, a woman may be afraid to touch her husband's body because she is frightened of hurting him. Relatives also find it hard to watch their loved one deteriorating physically and may show their distress by being over critical of the care given to the person. They may spend long periods with the care staff or talking to other relatives or clients. If a client has cancer, the pain of his relatives will demand as much of a care worker's time as her client does. If the care workers do not respond to them they may produce even more problems and demands.

DEMENTIA

Families and care workers looking after the client with dementia find it a difficult and frustrating job. He may be unpredictable and difficult to control, and need a lot of attention and supervision. The client's tendency to swing from rage to crying will leave his care givers emotionally exhausted by their attempts to deal with these extremes.

Many relatives experience the anticipatory grief described on page 31, that is, they begin to grieve for the loss of the person before his death. Relatives often spend hours describing the person the client used to be to the care worker. By retracing the client's life they are beginning the process of reevaluating what they had. This is a part of the grieving process.

One great sadness for many people is when they begin to lose their intellectual ability. It would be easy to assume that most people have little or no insight into what is happening to them, but this is not always the case. Care workers must be very careful not to talk about clients in front of them, as though they were unable to understand. Many clients, on losing intellectual function, become sad, angry and irritable. This may turn to depression when the finality of their loss is recognised. The client may go to great lengths to hide his impairment from family and friends. His shame and fear about losing control and being dependent on others reflects the enormity of the loss. This loss will be even more difficult for those who have valued their mental functions highly and seen them as central to their lives.

When a client with dementia is nearing the end of his life, the relatives may express relief and the hope that it will be over quickly. But they often believe that the care worker will pass judgement on them for having and expressing such feelings. Many talk about their guilt at feeling like this and it helps them to know that care workers accept and understand such feelings.

Grief and loss, and all the feelings associated with these conditions, can go on for years and be a tremendous burden for people. Recognising this, and giving relatives and friends a chance to share their feelings, is an important part of the care worker's role.

MISCARRIAGE

Spontaneous abortion occurs when a pregnancy is terminated naturally and may be called a 'miscarriage'. When spontaneous abortion is discussed with clients it is better to use the term miscarriage rather than abortion. Using 'miscarriage' avoids the connection with other types of abortion, such as elective abortion when a decision is made to deliberately end a pregnancy.

Miscarriage is not always recognised as a loss that produces significant grief. The strength of feeling resulting from the loss of a hoped-for child may or may not be affected by the length of the pregnancy. People may think that a pregnancy lost in the early weeks, before the fetus is considered viable (that is, sufficiently developed to be able to survive after birth), is less of a problem, but women who miscarry early do not usually agree with this view. Sometimes people try to reduce the pain of loss by saying things like, 'She's not had a chance to feel it moving yet,' but if the pregnancy has been accompanied by a desperate longing for children its loss is even more painfully felt.

The client may have had some signs of the approaching loss, such as a minimal vaginal bleed. If she had ignored these signs, or been told to rest and ignored the advice, the resulting loss can produce remorse, regret and anger. These feelings can be even stronger if the client has done all that was asked of her and still miscarried. She may begin to question the advice she was given and wonder if she could have done more. It is important that care workers do not immediately say 'Not at all- of course you aren't to blame.' The client needs to express her feelings. She may also feel guilty about such things as working too hard, continued sexual activity, smoking or alcohol consumption. Again, it is important to let the client 'talk out' these worries without quickly dismissing them as causes of the miscarriage.

If the woman has had a previous spontaneous abortion, and has taken extra measures to safeguard the fetus, she will feel angry and frustrated. In such cases, people often say something must have been wrong with the fetus so what happened was probably 'all for the best' but this is little comfort to most women in their loss and grief. It is also not very helpful to talk about possible future successful pregnancies, straight away. The client needs time to feel the loss of this pregnancy first, and then go through the grieving process, before considering another pregnancy.

A care worker's need to deal with the distress and pain of the loss quickly could be due to her own inability to stay with the pain. She must stay with the client's own pace. Women who have grieved for the loss of a fetus often feel bitter that people kept trying to explain away their pain.

CONTACT WITH THE DEAD PERSON

Everyone holds a different opinion about the value of contact with a person who has just died. You may have heard upsetting stories about the distress of people who were (often when they were children) dragged into a room and forced to kiss a dead person. Yet people who have sat with a dying person may find it valuable to return to see him or her a short time after the death, or the next day. This can provide confirmation of the death for them or give them another chance to say goodbye. Such visits are particularly important for relatives who were not present at the death. Although people occasionally regret seeing the body, most find it reassuring and comforting in the long run.

Care workers may be the ones who take people along to pay their last respects to a relative in their home, the hospital or in a chapel of rest. It is important that care workers do not suggest this makes them feel uncomfortable and that they would prefer not to do it; once the deceased has been buried or cremated any chance to see the person is gone for good.

The decision to prevent anyone from seeing a deceased person should not be taken lightly and some people say that care workers have no right to take it. Some people have been prevented from seeing the body, or have decided themselves not to see it, and have regretted it for the rest of their lives. Most people are able to deal with the reality of the way the body looks; if they are only able to imagine it they may think the worst.

Clients arriving to visit a dead person may value having some privacy to talk to the deceased. It is worthwhile suggesting that they might want to do this, as they may be embarrassed to ask for this time. People may also want to hold the deceased's hand but not know if this is allowed. As a care worker, you are in a position of greater strength than your clients at this time and you can ask if they would like to hold his hand.

Parents of stillborn babies are usually given the opportunity to hold and cuddle their child. Some hospitals offer the parents an opportunity to photograph the child or will arrange this for them. Again, as a care worker you can suggest this; by doing so you are acknowledging the existence of the child and allowing the parents to do so, both now and later.

53

Some families feel quite natural about visiting the deceased, either singly or in small groups which may include children. This usually has a positive outcome, but no one should be forced into viewing the deceased.

Viewing the dead person can be made the most natural thing to do and a way of saying goodbye. Facing up to the death and the start of separation from the person is part of the process we call grief. The other rituals covered in the last part of this chapter also help people to grieve.

Now try Exercise 20.

EXERCISE 20

You may have visited someone who has died to pay your last respects or say goodbye. If you have done so, can you remember what you saw and heard and whether there was a particular smell you associate with that visit?

Describe the surroundings, smells and sounds that were part of the experience. How did it compare with what you imagined?

It you have not had this experience you will only be able to imagine it. Your ideas may have been influenced by others, and by what you have seen on TV and in films.

Describe what you imagine the experience of visiting the dead might be like.

It is important that you confront your fears and imaginings about visiting a deceased person, however odd they may seem. Your fears can be very powerful and prevent the experience from being worthwhile.

FUNERALS AND RITUALS

"rites"

a form of behaviour with a fixed pattern, usually for religious purposes

All societies have their own funeral practices for the care and final disposal of a person's body. These funeral rites provide a formal structure for the expected behaviour of the bereaved and fulfill many of their needs.

RITUAL

Ritual involves ceremonies or customary acts which are often repeated in the same form. Ritual is often religious in nature and offers a reason for the death, or attempts to give it some meaning. A bereaved person may relive the funeral many times.

A GATHERING

By gathering together family and friends, the funeral provides people with an opportunity to give attention to the bereaved, recognise their loss and offer sympathy. This communication of caring is a useful form of social support. Wakes, viewings and visitations to the deceased and bereaved are gatherings of family and friends. Care workers and other health professionals perform similar functions when they review together what happened and share past experiences about the person who died.

PUBLIC ACKNOWLEDGEMENT

The funeral provides an opportunity to express the fact of the death publicly, finally ending at a place to dispose of the deceased. Accepting this fact with the body nearby (perhaps on display) brings to an end people's lives with the deceased. The formal end of a period in their lives helps people to accept the finality of the death and assists the process of grief.

The type of funeral, its size and the symbols like flowers which are used, also communicate to people the loss of the deceased to the community.

DISPOSAL OF THE BODY

Cremation, burial or entombment (or other methods, such as burial at sea) confront people with the fact that a life on earth has come to an end. For some people a headstone or scattering of ashes provides a place to which they can return for prayer, to reminisce (think about the past) or pay their respects to the deceased person. This part of the ritual also provides a healthy way to dispose of the body.

We have looked briefly at some of the functions of the funeral and the rites associated with it. All major life changes have rites surrounding them which help both individuals and society to adapt to the change. Baptisms, engagements and marriages are some other examples. Funerals offer this rite of the passage from life to death. They offer a way to emphasise the worth and value of the life of the deceased and to provide a testimony to the life he led.

During the funeral, the bereaved begin the process of severing the bonds between themselves and the deceased. This is the beginning of their adjustment to life without him and their movement towards a new state of existence. At the funeral, the bereaved appear in public without that person. They gradually become part of a different or changed social group and at the funeral they are declaring this change in public. The deceased is no longer a part of that group and the practices of cremation, burial or entombment are a very tangible expression of that.

The status of the deceased may be recognised at the funeral by certain rituals, such as a 21-gun salute, or uniformed colleagues from services such as the police, fire or ambulance being present or carrying the coffin.

Try Exercise 21

EXERCISE 21

Find out how someone arranges a secular funeral, that is, one which is not connected with a church or a particular religion.

What could happen at the ceremony, and how might it help people to grieve?

Funerals meet the needs of individual people mourning a loss and of society in general. They are for the living and offer spiritual, psychological and social benefits. Funerals are just as important for care workers, to help them accept an ending to a relationship; some care workers will need to attend the funeral. Care workers also need help to express in public the value they placed on the relationship and guidance about coming to terms with the end of that closeness. Care workers often accompany clients to funerals, too.

SUMMARY EXERCISES

Think about three other rituals – baptism, marriage and a civil ceremony for gay people.

List the changes that are being marked by these rituals. Many of the little incidents in life can cause us loss and grief.

The novelist George Eliot wrote, '*In every parting there is an image of death.*'

Next time you are in a railway station, airport or bus terminal, where people are leaving on journeys, make some observations.

Look for facial and body signs, and behaviours that show people are saying goodbye.

Describe what feelings and emotions are being expressed or how people are trying to hide (or suppress) them.

Make some observations of people waiting to welcome someone, before their arrival and again when they have met the person.

Conclusion

You may feel that the work discussed in this book involves only sadness, misery and pain. But loss and grief are part of everyday life and no one can avoid the strong feelings surrounding them. You may also think that you would prefer not to work with clients in such distressing situations because you would find it too upsetting or difficult. Yet care workers who do tackle the issues of loss and grief find the work very rewarding. They gain great insight into the nature of relationships and the ways in which people view life and give it meaning. Many care workers find that the challenge of working with loss and grief contributes to their own personal growth. They develop a clearer understanding of some of the different issues of life and gradually feel more comfortable with them.

Caring for those experiencing loss, grief and separation can make an obvious difference to people's lives, be a positive experience and make a useful and meaningful contribution to care. It is a privilege to share these significant milestones of life with people and it is not wrong to find that you actually enjoy the work.

We hope that this book has helped you to realise that many of these difficult events are more manageable than you thought, both for yourself and for the clients. Whatever the problems, the uniqueness of each event will make it an experience to value.

REFERENCES

Bowlby, J. 1981 *Sadness and depression: Attachment and loss,* vol 3. Penguin, Harmondsworth.

Branter, J.1977 *Positive approaches to dying: Death Education* (3) 293–304.

Freud, S. 1917 *Mourning and melancholia, standard edn.* vol XIV. Hogarth, London.

Gendlin, E. T., Beebe. J. 1968 'An experimental approach to group therapy' *Journal of Research and Development in Education,* 1: 19–29.

Kübler-Ross, E. 1969 *On death and dying.* Macmillan, New York.

Parkes, C. M. 1996, *Bereavement; studies of grief in adult life,* 2nd edn. Penguin, Harmondsworth.

Lindemann. E. 1944 'Symptomatology and Management of Acute Grief' *American Journal of Psychiatry* 101: 141–149.

SUGGESTED READING

Death and Bereavement by Dewi Rees. Published 2001, Whurr, London.

Grief in Children by Atle Dyregrov. Published 1990, Jessica Kingsley, London.

On Bereavement by Tony Walter. Published 1999, Open University Press, London.

Sudden Death by Bob Wright. Published 1999, Churchill Livingstone, Edinburgh.

Loss and Trauma edited by J.H. Harvey & E.D. Miller. Published 2000, Taylor & Francis Group, Sussex.

USEFUL ADDRESSES

Winston's Wish
The Clara Burgess Centre
Bayshill Road
Cheltenham
GL50 3AW
Tel: 01242 515157
Helpline: 0845 20 30 405
Help for grieving children and their families.

The Compassionate Friends
53 North Street
Bristol
BS3 1EN
Helpline: 0845 123 2304
For bereaved parents.

Cruse Bereavement Care
PO Box 800
Richmond
Surrey
TW9 1RG
Tel: 0208 939 9530
Helpline: 0844 477 9400

Macmillan Cancer Support
89 Albert Embankment
London
SE1 7UQ
Telephone helplines listed nationally

WAY Foundation
PO Box 6767
Brackley
NN13 6YW
Tel: 0870 011 3450
Widowed and young

Divorce care and support – local help on various websites.